vatch's thai street food

vatcharin bhumichitr

photography by Martin Brigdale
and Somchai Phongphaisarnkit

kyle cathie limited

for my brother, ed

First published in Great Britain in 2002 by
Kyle Cathie Limited
122 Arlington Road
London NW1 7HP
general.enquiries@kyle-cathie.com
www.kylecathie.com

ISBN 1 85626 402 5

1 3 5 7 9 8 6 4 2

Text © 2002 Vatcharin Bhumichitr
Food Photography © 2002 Martin Brigdale
Travel Photography © 2002 Somchai Phongphaisarnkit

Project Editor: Sheila Davies
Copy Editor: Catherine Ward
Editorial Assistant: Sarah Epton
Designer: Geoff Hayes
Home Economist: Linda Tubby
Stylist: Helen Trent
Production: Lorraine Baird and Sha Huxtable

Vatcharin Bhumichitr is hereby identified as the author of this
work in accordance with Section 77 of the Copyright, Designs
and Patents Act, 1988

A Cataloguing in Publication record for this title is available
from the British Library

Colour repro: Sang Choy International
Printed and bound in Singapore by Star Standard

**Woman selling sweetcorn
in front of the giant
chedi, Nakhon Pathom.**

contents

Anytime, Anywhere And Cheap

We heard them before we saw them, each with their unique sound. All manner of noises: the bong of a hand bell or the ping of a bicycle bell, the chock of wood striking a worn block, the clack of something like Spanish castanets or, the most obvious, the clang of a spoon against a pan. As greedy children we knew what, or rather whom, each noise represented, so we were ready for the spectacle that eventually ambled along our *soi*, the Thai word for the lanes that run off the *thanom*, or main city arteries. And what a spectacle it was as each vendor pulled, pushed or pedalled his customised storage box or cooking range past our house. The most common and simple was the *hahp*, a bamboo shoulder pole with rattan frames at each end holding baskets, evenly balanced so the vendor could pass down narrow alleyways or travel on the little boats from up-country villages into the city early every morning. Some just brought fruit and vegetables straight from their farms, while others came with ready-prepared dishes or the wherewithal to cook them. You could often see a slim young lady or a wizened old grandmother kneeling on the ground beside her *hahp*, but if you tried to lift it you'd be surprised at how heavy it was – they could carry amazing weights. You still see them everywhere – by the river or crossing busy city intersections. They

Woman selling grilled sausages and other north-eastern specialities at the night food market, Surin.

are the moving restaurants of Asia, and are so important there is even a proverb about them: 'a broken *hahp* is like a broken home'. Another common spectacle in our soi was the pushcart or tricycle cart, a simple variant of the bicycle pushing a large wheeled box containing everything needed to make delicious food.

We children didn't care how the food arrived – we just wanted lots of it, so when we heard the bell or the block we would rush out and order noodles or sweets or ice-cream before our mothers could stop us. We knew what many tourists have learned since, that this was the most convenient, the freshest and cheapest food available.

If you want a street vendor, you'll find clusters of them at any market, bus or train terminal, or near busy city office blocks. There are also special food areas in all the major city centres – anyone will tell you where. The food is great because vendors specialise in one dish, often grow their own ingredients or get them fresh from that day's market and use classic country recipes – which is the point of this book. These are the basic recipes of Thai cuisine, which because they have to be made on the move, are usually very easy to cook.

We children loved the street food sellers and, by the time our mothers caught up with us, the cooking would be started and they would have to pay. Naturally, this would annoy them very much but there was nothing they could do. Until, that is, the arrival of See Ooey. This gruesome character came from China and, starting in the south of Thailand, worked his way north, kidnapping and murdering children on the way. He would wait down a quiet lane for the food vendors to pass and then pounce. Horrible as it was, it was a gift for our mothers who would call 'See Ooey will get you if you go out', which stopped us for a while. I don't know the full story, but the tale was even embellished with threats that See Ooey ate his victims. Eventually they caught him near Rayong on the coast east of Bangkok. He confessed and was condemned to death without any problem. There is a grizzly souvenir of those days in the Siriraj Hospital, where his remains are pickled and on display. I understand that tourists can visit them in some sort of

A typical *hahp* food seller, the most common form of street food in Thailand.

ghoulish tour. At the time it only interfered with our eating habits, though it meant more to my youngest brother who is also called Ooey and so was given a hard time at school by the other boys.

Street food really is the lifeline of Asia, helping feed millions of people daily. The first European tourists, the backpackers, hanging around Kow San Road (the street featured in the film 'The Beach') discovered it was a cheap and delicious way to eat. They soon turned Kow San Road into a food market and open-air restaurant and began the process of popularising Thai food, which has now spread around the world. Curiously enough, today the whole business is reversed with Bangkokians going to eat in Kow San Road because the food is good and they get a free cabaret staring at the crazy antics of the young foreigners.

Street food is always on the move, not just down narrow lanes but also in entire urban areas. In the rapidly expanding cities of Asia, with their ever-shifting centres of activity, from banking to tourism, it is the ability of street vendors to speedily adapt to changes that makes them so essential to the well-being of millions of people. When I was young, the streets around Pratunam (the Watergate), near to what was then Bangkok's main modern shopping area, were lined with food sellers, not only during shop opening hours but also at night when young people would meet up after a show or a club or just to enjoy a bowl of noodles in the cooler night air. Many a love affair began on the tiny stools clustered round Pratunam's food stalls. Today, things have moved on. There are newer, more exciting, shopping centres and all that remains at the once famous Pratunam is the seafood market opposite the Amari Watergate Hotel.

By contrast, a totally new food area sprang up when the Bangkok Bank opened its new headquarters on Silom (windmill) Road. No doubt many of the vendors from Pratunam also moved to what is now one of the city's largest open-air restaurants clustered at the foot of the bank's building, serving not only the clerks and managers from the bank but the hundreds of workers in what has become the hub of the city's financial district. One can see different examples of this adaptability around the country.

Because of the oppressive heat in Surin, a major town in the once isolated northeastern province of Isan, street food sellers have turned night into day.

Street food becomes a restaurant in the night food market, Surin.

To most tourists, Surin is only on the map because of the famous large-scale once-yearly elephant round-up, or the elephant training village at nearby Ban Ta Klang, but Surin is worth a visit to see the equally large-scale night market. A typical trader is a woman I spoke to, who was making the famous Isan spicy salad *Som Tam*, which has now spread all over Thailand. She turns up at 9pm and is bent over her large stone mortar, pounding grated papaya, nuts and chillies, well into the night. Her regular spot is on the Thanon Krung Sri Nai, a long street in the town centre that has the regular town market for fruit, vegetables and spices at one end and what is effectively a huge open-air restaurant of street food sellers at the other. Because of the heat, the market suppliers deliver during the night and the shoppers come at dawn. The food sellers feed the traders during the dark hours, the shoppers at first-light, and even provide suppers for late-night diners. They cluster in groups offering a range of dishes and transform themselves into restaurants with small tables and stools. Children will run and get beers and soft drinks from nearby shops. The whole place is brightly lit with coloured neon strips and buzzing with excitement. I last visited during the rainy season and it was like a swimming pool, but still fascinating. A typical customer is Khun Patcharin, the brother of a friend of mine in England, who cultivates oyster mushrooms and delivers them to the market at 2am. He then chooses his food seller and has his main meal of the day. Actually, he is surrounded by street food – his farm is near a famous beauty spot, the town's main reservoir, which attracts people by its fresher air and where street sellers come to provide instant picnics. This is a key point, that in Thailand you don't need a street to have street food. You can find it anywhere – on beaches and by rivers and highways, on railway station platforms as well as in the train carriages.

Street sellers are very ingenious. They know, for example, that most drivers leave Bangkok around 8am, so they cluster at the point where the average driver will be on any road at about midday, ready for lunch. This is particularly noticeable as you drive across the invisible provincial border into Isan itself, where you suddenly start to see large model chickens by the roadside which indicate that there are food vendors selling the famous *Gai Yang* barbecued chicken. Every place has its local specialities. On popular beaches on the Gulf Coast west of Bangkok, like those at Cha-am and Hua Hin, food sellers with their *hahps* or trays ceaselessly parade with seafood and shellfish or gather in clusters making open-air beach restaurants, where squid and prawns are grilled and mussels steamed. Thais expect to find special food everywhere and an impromptu picnic is often the main reason for visiting somewhere.

One of the biggest food areas in the country is in a town not far from Bangkok called Nakhon Pathom, renowned for its giant *chedi* or bell-shaped temple, which is one of the largest Buddhist monuments in the world and certainly the largest in Thailand. All the streets around it are full of food stalls and at its base is a vast open-air restaurant which is as much street theatre as food supplier – vendors toss balls of ice-cream in the air and catch them in cornets for enchanted children, cake sellers display sweets in every colour of the rainbow. It really doesn't have very much to do with pure Buddhism, which counsels restraint in everything, but to see such excess is certainly worth a day out.

Because they are such convenient one-dish meals, you find many street food vendors selling the same dishes all over Thailand. Nevertheless, I've divided this book into the five main food areas of the country because some important differences still remain. While it is true that food vendors congregating in and around the capital have given Bangkok and its surrounding region the most varied menu in the country, it is also the most strongly influenced by Chinese cuisine. Regionally, the greatest differences come from the influence of neighbouring countries and the use of local ingredients – Malaysia and seafood in the south, Burma and rich sauces in the north, Laos and plentiful charcuterie in the northeast. There is a straight split between the centre and the south, where conventional paddy rice is the staple, and the north and northeast, where sticky or glutinous rice is preferred. You'll find all these differences reflected in this book.

One of the traditional places to find street food is along the rivers and *klongs*, the canals that criss-cross the country. Worth a visit is the former capital, Ayutthaya, a city of canals with sensational ruins and monuments. Here you will find many fine floating restaurants as well as traditional *Gueyteow Rua*, or noodle boats, which still pass up and down its waterways. I like to go to Ayutthaya's Patuchai area, where they sell *Roti Si Mi* (silk threads), a pancake stuffed with sweet noodles that look like fine hair – hence the name. I don't give the recipe because it's far too complicated, but it's well worth walking along the street in Ayutthaya to see the noodle makers tease out the ball of wheat flour, sugar and water into fine threads so quickly they seem like magicians. Extraordinarily, they are all Muslims who at some point travelled from the south looking for work. I talked to Bang Somboom Arun, who does a sort of roadside show with his son who is learning the trade. Bang Somboon's brother travelled first to Bangkok, where he eventually settled and met a Vietnamese woman who taught him to make the threads, a Vietnamese speciality. He didn't have a shop, so he walked the streets selling the filled pancakes out of two brass tins carried on his back like two biscuit tins with open windows set in them so people could see what he was offering. Bang Somboon joined him and took over the business while his brother went on to make *Kow Mok Gai*, a Muslim chicken dish. Bang Somboon is just one of a large Muslim community in Ayutthaya, proof of how street food unites the country. He still has his brother's brass tins, but he has settled down on a fixed site now where people come to him.

Many of the street sellers are poor people who want to make a living for themselves, a widow, perhaps, who is left without any resources except her ability to cook, or a young man with limited education. They start by carrying

The author buying a palm fruit beside the motorway from Bangkok to Petchaburi.

their *hahps* around, progress to a pushcart, then hope to find a fixed spot with other food sellers and eventually grow to a roadside restaurant, employing other people. Thailand abounds with stories of people who have made it rich this way. My brother Ed was eating at a stall in Yaowarat, Bangkok's Chinatown, famous for its food, when he heard one of the boys who was serving say to his brother: 'Mother's tired now, go and get the Mercedes'. He pointed to the Chinese woman who was cooking at a steaming pot in the corner. Sure enough, it wasn't a joke. A Mercedes duly appeared and they started packing up. She had made her money, but was too superstitious to break her luck by giving up what had brought her good fortune. Near to the Grand Palace in Bangkok, a woman called Khun Pa Ni Chiapchalaart used to sell *Khao Niew Manuang* (Sticky Rice with Mango). She now has a famous shop selling the best sweet rice and succulent mangoes and people make pilgrimages to buy them.

Food vendors come into their own at special occasions, particularly temple celebrations and village fairs. Two of the biggest are not yet on the regular tourist circuit, but well worth a visit. The village of Ban Ta Klang, near Surin in northeastern Thailand, is famous for training elephants. It's full of them and they wander around free and friendly. In fact, the village is often referred to simply as Moo Bahn Chang (elephant village). It's near the border with Cambodia and most of the people, who speak Khmer, treat the elephants as part of the family – they show respect to them like grandfathers and grandmothers because they have such long lives. In April or May just before the rains come, the men finish studying or farming and spend a short time in the local temple as novice monks. At the monk-making ceremony, the men's heads are shaved, they are dressed in white and made up in bright colours and carried to the temple in an enormous procession of brightly caparisoned elephants which wends its way from the river Mae Nam

Wang Ta. Look through the village to the monastery and you will find long lines of food stalls, which have been set up to feed the hundreds of visitors who come to see the great spectacle. The elephants often help themselves to titbits as they amble along.

It's the same in Chiang Mai at about the same time, when they hold the Inthakhin Festival. The Inthakhin Pillar, which is kept at Wat Chedi Luang, is not really a simple pillar, but a phallic fertility symbol, a survivor of the old animist beliefs that preceded Buddhism. It is sacred to most northerners who come to pray for abundant rains and a plentiful harvest at the May/June festival. Thousands of people take part in the week long festival. Young boys in ancient military uniforms parade around and the food is very special, with the vendors dressing up in historical costumes trying to sell authentic food from the past.

It would be wrong to imagine that with modern urban life street food will disappear. While it is true that the new shopping malls and department stores attract many city customers with their giant food halls, these places actually use the same principle as the street food open-air restaurants and effectively, it is street food moved indoors. Both are simply lines of individual cooks, each specialising in one particular dish. Street food really is the best type of cuisine and I have been gathering these recipes on the lanes, highways, rivers and beaches of Thailand since I was that greedy little boy. My favourite meal is still when I find a crowded market in a new place, pick a street vendor and eat something local that I haven't tried before. I hope this book helps you share some of my experiences.

Bang Somboon Arun making 'silk threads' (*Roti Si Mi*).

before you begin

Equipment

The average Western kitchen should have all the equipment necessary for these recipes, although it would be an advantage to have a large mortar and pestle. You will also need a steamer (see page 29).

Amounts and measurements

The quantities given for each dish (unless otherwise stated) will provide enough for a light snack for two people if eaten on its own, or enough for four if part of a larger meal with other dishes.

All ingredient quantities are given in both metric and imperial measures. Do not alternate between the two as they are not interchangable, and doing so might jeopardise the result.

Ingredients

1 Thai cooks do not go by measurements but by flavour, so you should always sample everything and adjust the amounts I have given to suit your personal taste. The quantities here could be thought of as average, but more or less of anything, chillies or fish sauce for example, can be used, if desired.

2 It is also best to remember that vegetables in Asia tend to be smaller than those in Europe or America, so try not to select giant bulbous specimens when shopping for these ingredients. Chilli and garlic always have a more intense flavour in Asia than in the West so you may find you like to adjust their quantities accordingly.

3 As a general principle, everything should be cut into bite-sized pieces (as we seldom use knives at the table), and always under- rather than over-cook.

4 Even tinned goods tend to vary, particularly coconut milk, which can be thicker or thinner depending on the brand (some add flour to thicken it). As I cannot list every supplier here, it is a good idea to try a few varieties and choose your own individual favourites.

5 With fish it is important to know that Thais like to deep-fry the whole fish until it is quite hard, then eat everything including any little bones. I have given Thai cooking times, but if you like your fish more moist and with the bones removed you will need to adjust the cooking time accordingly.

6 Overall, you must remember that a Thai cook works more by intuition than measurement and you too should follow this system to some extent when cooking Thai food for yourself. If it tastes good, go with it.

Holy basil.

fresh ingredients

Aubergine

Four varieties of aubergine are used in southeast Asian cuisine, two soft and two hard. The soft aubergines are the large purple/black aubergine familiar in the West, and the long, thin pink-skinned aubergine. The hard ones include the small, round, green aubergine, about 2.5cm (1in) in diameter, and the pea aubergine, also green and rather like an inflated garden pea. These last two will only be available in specialist oriental stores.

Banana leaf

Although not really a cooking ingredient, banana leaves are often used in Thailand to serve food on and to wrap up parcels of food before steaming or grilling. Cooking food in banana leaves gives it a slight but distinctive flavour, but if you can't get hold of them, tin foil is an adequate substitute. Bamboo and lotus leaves are also used in this way but are probably even harder to get hold of in the West.

Basil

Sweet basil (*bai horabha*),the variety most commonly found in Europe, has shiny green leaves tinged with purple and a smell tinged with cinnamon and cloves. It is cooked at the last minute or used fresh as a garnish. Holy or Thai basil (*bai krapow*) has narrower, slightly hairy leaves, a stronger taste and it must be cooked.

Chilli

Three varieties are used in this book: small fresh red or green chillies (*prik khee noo*) about 2.5cm (1in) long and fiery; medium fresh red or green chillies (*prik chee faa*), finger length, about 7.5cm (3in) long and less hot; and large dried red chillies (*prik haeng*) about 7.5cm (3in) long and medium heat.

Pea aubergines and the larger hard green aubergines.

Young ginger.

Chinese celery (*kunchai*)

This is similar to Western celery, but has looser stems, a smaller diameter and a much stronger flavour, which means some adjustment if you substitute another variety. Choose those with the fattest and whitest stalks, as these will be the most tender. Chop them more finely than you would with Western celery as they can be stringy.

Coriander (*pak chee*)

Closely resembling Italian or flat-leaf parsley, fresh coriander leaves are used as a garnish. The root and/or stalk is usually crushed to make a paste or chopped and added as a cooking ingredient. Roots and stalks can be frozen.

Galangal (*khaa*)

This creamy-white rhizome is slightly harder than ginger. It is used in the same way, but has a more lemony flavour.

Ginger (*king*)

Knobbly, golden-beige 'fingers' of fresh ginger are now readily available from supermarkets, but are often old or musty. Try to buy the young roots (rhizomes) which are pinker in colour. Well-wrapped, fresh ginger can be kept for up to two weeks in a refrigerator. It also freezes well and can be grated from frozen.

Kaffir lime, see *lime*

'Lesser' garlic (*krachai*)

This long, straight, thin rhizome has a slightly lemony, gingery flavour. It should be peeled and is prepared in the same way as ginger. It can be bought from oriental shops.

Lemon grass (*takrai*)

This widely used herb is sold as long lemony scented blades, always with the leaves chopped off. Try to buy pale-green, near white, bulbous stalks, roughly 23cm (9in) long. If they are old, you will need to peel away the hard outer leaves down to the tender centre. When cooked, lemon grass imparts a fresh citrus taste with a touch of ginger, but without the bitter acidity of lemon or lime. Rings of chopped lemon grass can be frozen and used directly from the freezer.

Lime (*manao*)

Little green limes are the most common citrus flavouring in southeast Asian cooking. Lemons can be substituted at a pinch. Where kaffir lime (*bai magrut*) is specified, it is usually the lime leaves that are needed, which add tang, or the skin or zest, which has a strong citrus punch. To shred lime leaves, pile them on top of one another, then roll them into a 'cigarette' and cut them across in very thin slices to produce fine slivers of leaf.

Long bean (*tua ffak yow*)

At up to a metre (3ft) in length, the aptly named long bean resembles a wildly overgrown string bean (which can be used as a substitute). The long bean, however, is crunchier and cooks faster. Choose darker beans with small bean seeds inside the pods.

Mooli, see *white radish*

Morning glory/water spinach (*pak boong*)

With a slight flavour of Western spinach, the long jointed stems of this water vegetable remain firm when cooked, while the arrow-shaped leaves quickly go limp. The leaves will turn yellow and go off if not used promptly.

Mushroom

Dried fungus mushrooms (cloud ears) are the most common Asian mushroom. They are usually black, but there is a white variety. Both are easily available and are usually bought in 60g (2oz) packets. They should be soaked at room temperature until soft (20–30 minutes), then checked to see that no sandy grit remains. The smaller they are the better. Readily available Western varieties which you can use instead include the champignon or button mushroom, the large flat parasol mushroom and the straw mushroom, which is slightly more pointed than the button mushroom, as well as the oyster or pleurotte mushroom.

Papaya/pawpaw (*malako*)

This large, green gourd-like fruit with soft yellow-orange flesh is eaten like melon. When unripe and still green, the hard flesh is grated and used as a vegetable.

Taro (*pooak*)

This large, oval tuber, which needs to be peeled, is cooked in the same way as potato. It can be found in Indian or Oriental shops.

Turmeric (*khamin*)

Brown and flaky on the outside, bright orange-yellow on the inside, this rhizome adds a warm, spicy taste but is mostly used dried and ground to add colour. Fresh turmeric is now more widely available in the West, but only buy small amounts. Treat fresh turmeric like ginger: cut off a small section, peel it, then chop or pound it according to the instructions in the recipe.

Water spinach, see *morning glory*

White radish (*mooli*)

This long, white root vegetable, with a cool sharpness when raw, is a bit like turnip when cooked. It can also be found in Japanese stores, where it is known as daikon.

Bamboo shoot.

the storecupboard

Bamboo shoot (*normai*)

The 'shoot' is the first soft stage of the bamboo when it appears out of the ground, before it hardens into the cane. The shoot has to be stripped of its needle-sharp hairs and boiled to remove the bitter, poisonous acid. Don't worry, though, even in Asia bamboo shoots are bought ready-prepared by experts and in the West they are always bought tinned. They can be divided into 'spring' shoots and 'winter' shoots, the latter being considered the more tender and sweet. Unfortunately, the tins seldom indicate which variety is contained. Tinned in brine, they are yellowish in colour and after opening may be kept in water in a sealed container in a refrigerator for several days.

Beancurd (*tofu*)

Blocks of white fresh beancurd are sold in plastic trays, in a little of their own milky liquid, usually divided into nine cubes. They are best used on the day of purchase, but may be kept for up to three days in a refrigerator, provided the liquid is poured away each day and replaced with fresh water. Cubes of deep-fried beancurd are usually available in oriental shops, but deep-frying your own fresh beancurd until it is golden brown, produces something so superior that I strongly recommend making the extra effort.

Beancurd sheets (*fong tao hou*)

These are sold dried in packets. They are quite fragile but will separate easily if soaked for 5–6 minutes. Torn sections can be patched with other sheets.

Bean sauce (*tow jiew*)

This is made from mashed and fermented soya beans – black or yellow. Black bean sauce is thick with a rich flavour; yellow bean sauce is more salty and pungent. Black bean sauce is most commonly used.

Chilli oil

One method of making chilli oil involves first grilling dried chillies with fresh garlic and shallots, then pounding them to a paste and stir-frying in oil to give a powerful, hot flavour. Another method involves frying the dried chillies, garlic and shallots in oil until crisp, then pounding and stir-frying. You can make chilli oil yourself (see page 26), but many people prefer to buy it ready-made in bottles. Each country has its own version and there is little difference between them. You will only need quite small amounts, but it will keep, well-sealed, in a refrigerator for at least a year.

Chilli powder (*prik pon*)

This red powder, made by grinding small dried red chillies, is sold in jars, tins, packets or cardboard containers.

Coconut milk or cream

Buy this in tins. The thin liquid that collects at the top of the tin (before it is shaken or stirred) is called coconut milk. After stirring or shaking, the thick liquid is called coconut cream. It's as simple as that!

Dried shrimps (*gung haeng*)

These tiny sun-dried shrimps, sold loose or in jars or plastic bags, will keep for a long time. They are not meant to be reconstituted by soaking in water, but are used as flavouring. Choose those that are not too pink or salty. See *shrimp paste*.

Fish ball (*louchin pla*) **and Fish cake**

Both the fish and flour dumplings and the cake can be bought ready-made from oriental shops. They are already cooked and simply need re-heating.

Fish sauce (*nam pla*)

The 'salt' of southeast Asia, this liquid – extracted from fermented fish – is the principal savoury taste in nearly all the recipes in this book. The best fish sauce is young, with a light whisky colour and a refreshingly salty taste; the worst is old, dark and bitter. The easiest to find are those from Thailand (*nam pla*) or Vietnam (*nuoc mam*). The amount of fish sauce in a dish is clearly a matter of taste. I have prescribed modest quantities, so taste and add more if you wish. Strict vegetarians, who do not eat fish, should substitute light soy sauce, bearing in mind that it is less salty so more will be needed.

Jasmine flower water

This can be bought ready-made, or you can make it yourself by soaking 10 jasmine flowers in 400ml (14fl oz) water for about an hour.

Lotus seeds

These preserved seeds are available from oriental stores.

Moong/Mung beans

These small, yellow dried beans are often used in desserts and need to be pre-soaked to soften them. Available from oriental shops.

Oil

As a general rule, southeast Asian cookery demands a neutral-flavoured vegetable oil both for cooking or as an ingredient. In Thailand, oil used to be made by frying pig fat over a low heat. This is now considered to be very unhealthy and most Thais today use plain vegetable oil. Flavours are often added by frying garlic or shallots in the oil at the beginning of the cooking process. There are occasional exceptions: some Chinese-based dishes require sesame oil for its rich flavour; other dishes come from territories that produce a particularly flavourful nut oil (generally peanut, which is most commonly sold here as groundnut oil), which colours the dish. Uniquely for Asia, the Filipinos, under the heavy influence of Spain, have taken to using olive oil for some of their dishes, especially salads. For all other countries in the region, however, olive and other distinctively flavoured oils, should be strictly avoided.

Palm sugar (*nam tan peep*)

This is made from the sap of the coconut palm. It is sold in compressed cakes which keep well. The best is soft and brown and has a rich toffee-like aroma. Usually used in desserts, it is an essential ingredient if you want the full caramel taste of some southeast Asian dishes. Dark demerara sugar is a possible, but poor, substitute. Available from oriental shops.

Pickled cabbage (*pak gat dong*)

Small pieces of firm white cabbage preserved in boiled vinegar, salt and sugar for at least three days. It is served as a relish or cooked and added, as a salty, slightly sour ingredient, to a variety of dishes.

Pickled garlic (*kratium dong*)

Normally this is bought ready-prepared in a jar, but you can make it yourself if you wish. Soak 450g (1lb) whole garlic cloves (unpeeled) in a bowl of cold water for one hour, then drain and pull away the skins. Leave the cloves to dry for an hour. In the meantime, heat 225ml (8fl oz) rice vinegar in a heavy-based saucepan, add 225g (8oz) sugar and two tablespoons salt. Dissolve over a low heat, then leave to cool. Place the garlic in a preserving jar, pour over the cold liquid, close tightly and leave for at least one month before using.

Pickled garlic (right) and tamarind pods (above, right).

Pork ball (*louchin moo*)

This is a pork and flour dumpling, bought ready-made in oriental shops.

Preserved plum (*bue dong*)

This is sold preserved in syrup in oriental shops and is used to make sweet plum sauce.

Preserved radish, turnip or other vegetable

Chi po is preserved white radish or mooli and *tang chi* is made from a variety of hard vegetable stems, most often cabbage. In both cases, the vegetable is mashed with salt and allowed to 'sweat'. After several repeats and a sun-drying process, the preserved vegetables are packed into sealed jars or plastic bags and sold in oriental shops. Only small slivers are needed to enhance the flavour of a dish.

Shrimp paste (*kapee*)

This dark purple paste has a formidable smell that disappears on cooking and adds a rich pungent taste to any dish. Store in a tightly sealed jar or risk a malodorous kitchen. See dried shrimps.

Soy sauce (*siew*)

This is made from soya beans. Light soy sauce is light coloured, almost clear, with a delicately salty taste. Dark soy sauce is thicker and stronger and used mainly to add colour to a dish.

Spring roll sheets

These paper-thin pastry wrappers can be bought ready-made in packets from oriental shops and some supermarkets.

Tamarind (*makham*)

The pulp extracted from the pods of the tamarind tree is used to impart a pungent, sour, lemony flavour. Buy it in compressed blocks. Most recipes call for it to be dissolved in water to make 'tamarind water' or 'liquid'. Place a lump of tamarind, roughly equivalent to a heaped tablespoon, in warm water and knead it until the water is deep brown and all the flavour has been extracted.

Vinegar

While rice vinegar would be authentic, usually any plain light white wine vinegar can be substituted.

Won ton pastry

This is available in pre-cut sheets from oriental shops. Unlike spring roll wrappers, which are white in colour, these are yellow.

Water chestnuts

These small, sweet and juicy tubers add a crunchy texture to a dish. They are sold in tins in oriental shops and some supermarkets.

rice

Sticky or glutinous rice (*khao niew*)

Nearly always served with northern Thai or Lao food, this is a broad short-grain rice, mostly white but sometimes brown or black. When cooked, it is thick and slightly porridgey in texture and can be rolled into a ball and used as a scoop for other food. Sadly, it cannot be cooked in an electric rice-steamer.

To cook 450g (1lb) sticky rice, cover in water and soak for at least 3 hours, preferably overnight. Drain and rinse thoroughly. Line the perforated part of a steamer with double thickness muslin or cheesecloth and place the rice on top. Bring the water in the bottom of the steamer to the boil and steam the rice over a moderate heat for 30 minutes.

sweet sticky rice balls

Sticky rice is also used in puddings. In this recipe, the sticky rice is formed into balls and dipped in sugar syrup.

225g (8oz) cooked sticky rice
food dyes (optional)
675g (1¹/₂lb) granulated sugar
350ml (12fl oz) water

Divide the rice and dip it in different food dyes as fancy dictates. Place the sugar and water in a heavy-based saucepan and dissolve the sugar over a low heat. Bring to the boil and boil rapidly to form a thick syrup. Remove from the heat. Take small handfuls of the coloured rice and form it into rice balls, then dip into the sugar syrup. Remove with a slotted spoon and place on a metal tray to harden.

noodles

There are five varieties of noodle commonly used in Thailand. You can buy most of these fresh in oriental shops, but it is more likely that you will find them dried. All dried noodles, with the exception of *ba mee* noodles, need to be soaked in cold water for about 20 minutes before cooking (*wun sen* noodles require slightly less time). The dry weight will usually double after soaking, thus 100g (4oz) dry noodles will produce about 225g (8oz) soaked noodles. After soaking they should be drained before cooking. To cook, dunk them in boiling water for 2–3 seconds or stir-fry according to the recipe.

Sen yai
Sometimes called 'rice river noodle' or 'rice stick', this is a broad, flat, white rice flour noodle. Usually bought fresh, when it is rather sticky and needs to be separated before cooking, but it can also be bought dried.

Sen mee
A small, wiry-looking rice flour noodle, usually sold dried and sometimes called 'rice vermicelli'.

Sen lek
A medium-sized rice flour noodle, usually sold dried. The city of Chanthaburi is famous for *sen lek* noodles, which are sometimes called 'Jantaboon noodles' after the nickname for the town.

Ba mee
An egg and rice flour noodle, medium-yellow in colour, which comes in a variety of shapes, each with its own name. It is very unlikely that you will see anything other than the commonest form, which is thin and spaghetti-like, curled up in 'nests' that need to be shaken loose before cooking.

Wun sen
A very thin, very wiry, translucent soya bean flour noodle, also called 'vermicelli' or 'cellophane' noodle. Only available dried.

the four flavours kruang prung

While each noodle dish has its own distinctive taste, the final flavour is left to the diner, who can adjust the taste by sprinkling on quite small amounts of the Four Flavours. These are always put out in little serving bowls whenever noodles are served. The flavours are:

1 Chillies in fish sauce (*nam pla prik*): 4 small fresh red or green chillies, finely chopped, in 4 tablespoons fish sauce.

2 Chillies in rice vinegar (*prik nam som*): 4 small fresh red or green chillies, finely chopped, in 4 tablespoons rice vinegar.

3 Sugar (*nam tan*)

4 Chilli powder (*prik pon*)

prepared sauces

Curry and chilli pastes

There are five curry or chilli pastes used frequently in Thai cooking. Many can now be bought ready-made in oriental shops or even tinned in Western supermarkets. If you would like to make your own, here are the recipes:

green curry paste gaeng kiow wan

2 long fresh green chillies, chopped

10 small fresh green chillies, chopped

2 tablespoons chopped lemon grass

4 shallots, chopped

2 tablespoons chopped garlic

2.5cm (1in) piece galangal, chopped (see page 17)

1 teaspoon ground coriander seed

1 tablespoon chopped coriander root

1 teaspoon chopped kaffir lime skin or finely chopped leaves

2 teaspoons shrimp paste (see page 21)

1/2 teaspoon ground cumin

1/2 teaspoon ground white pepper

1 teaspoon salt

Using a pestle and mortar, blend all the ingredients together to form a smooth paste. This recipe should make about 4 tablespoons (60ml) paste.

red curry paste gaeng pet

8 long driedred chillies, de-seeded and chopped

1 teaspoon ground coriander seed

1/2 teaspoon ground cumin seed

1 teaspoon ground white pepper

2 tablespoons chopped garlic (about 4 cloves)

2 stalks lemon grass, finely chopped

3 coriander roots, chopped

1 teaspoon chopped kaffir lime skin or finely chopped leaves

2.5cm (1in) piece galangal, chopped (see page 17)

2 teaspoons shrimp paste (see page 21)

1 teaspoon salt

Using a pestle and mortar, blend all the ingredients to make a smooth paste. This recipe should make about 4 tablespoons (60ml) paste.

dry curry paste panaeng

10 long dried red chillies, de-seeded and chopped

5 shallots, chopped

2 tablespoons chopped garlic (about 4 cloves)

2 stalks lemon grass, chopped

2.5cm (1in) piece galangal, chopped (see page 17)

1 teaspoon ground coriander seed

1 teaspoon ground cumin seed

3 coriander roots, chopped

1 teaspoon shrimp paste (see page 21)

2 tablespoons roasted peanuts

Using a pestle and mortar, blend all the ingredients together to form a smooth paste. This recipe should make about 6 tablespoons (90ml) paste.

massaman paste massaman

10 long dried red chillies, de-seeded and chopped

1 tablespoon ground coriander seed

1 teaspoon ground cumin seed

1 teaspoon ground cinnamon

1 teaspoon ground cloves

1–2 star anise

1 teaspoon ground cardamom

1 teaspoon ground white pepper

4 tablespoons chopped shallots (about 6 shallots)

4 tablespoons chopped garlic (about 7 cloves)

about 5cm (2in) piece lemon grass, chopped

1cm (1/2in) piece galangal, chopped (see page 17)

1 tablespoon chopped kaffir lime skin or finely chopped lime leaves

1 tablespoon shrimp paste (see page 21)

1 tablespoon salt

Blend the chillies, coriander, cumin, cinnamon, cloves, star anise, cardamom and white pepper together in a pestle and mortar. Add the rest of the ingredients, one by one, blending after each addition, until you have a smooth paste. This recipe should make about 6 tablespoons (90ml) paste.

grilled chilli oil
tom yam sauce (nam prik pao)

5 garlic cloves, peeled

5 shallots, peeled

5 long dried red chillies, de-seeded and chopped

4 tablespoons vegetable oil

2 teaspoons sugar

1 teaspoon salt

1 tablespoon ground dried shrimps

1 Place the garlic, shallots and dried red chillies on a piece of foil and set under a preheated grill, turning occasionally with tongs, until the skins start to blister and become charred.

2 Using a pestle and mortar, pound together to make a paste.

3 In a small frying pan, heat the oil and add the paste. Stir a couple of times in the hot oil, then add the sugar, salt and ground dried shrimps. Cook for 5 minutes, stirring all the time.

cooking techniques

Boiling meat

We have a way of cooking chicken or duck breast that ensures they are neither tough nor overcooked. Place the breast in a pan, just cover with cold water, bring to the boil then remove from the heat. Cover with the pan lid and leave in the boiled water for 10 minutes, until just cooked through.

Crisp-frying

To add flavour and a crunchy texture to a dish, some ingredients – such as dried shrimps, chopped garlic and shallots, and shredded lime leaf – are fried in hot oil until they crisp up.

Dry-frying

Again to add flavour and a crunchy texture to a dish, ingredients like grated coconut, uncooked rice grains, sesame seeds (white or black) and sunflower seeds are placed in a frying pan without oil and heated until they darken and release their aroma. Sesame seeds will jump around as they warm up.

Deep-frying

Spring rolls, banana fritters and pork toasts are all deep-fried. It is easiest to use a deep-frier, set to a temperature of 200°C (400°F), but you can also use a deep saucepan set over a high heat. Vegetable oil is generally used.

Grinding or powdering

Dry-fried ingredients can be ground to a powder in a mortar. This will impart the same flavour as the whole dry-fried ingredients, but will give the dish a different, smoother texture. Dried shrimps can also be ground to a fine white powder, but you can buy them ready-ground in packets.

Steaming

This method is used for cooking sticky rice and a number of other recipes. Either use a traditional Chinese bamboo steamer or improvise with a large saucepan, using an upturned heatproof bowl to support a plate above the boiling water in the pan.

Stir-frying

This is always done very quickly over a very high heat. Oil is added to a hot wok and when it begins to form a haze, the ingredients are tossed in – garlic first, to flavour the oil, followed in turn by meat, noodles, sauce and then vegetables. These are stirred and turned rapidly over a high heat until the hardest ingredients are just cooked and still crunchy. Stir-fries should be eaten straight away.

bangkok

Early travellers visiting Bangkok recorded how the Thais lived both beside the water and in it – so close was their relationship to the river and the interconnected network of canals that made up the city's main highways. These water dwellers, living in stilt houses half in and half out the water, received all their supplies by boat, including their meals. Noodle boats (*rhua*), whose sellers floated along with a heater to boil the water for the noodles and a pan in which to cook the sauce, can still be seen today on many canals that secretly exist behind the tall buildings. This is the original street food of Thailand – water-born street food – and most visitors catch a glimpse of it at the famous floating market on the outskirts of modern Bangkok.

thai fried noodles with prawns pad thai gung

When I was young, one of the attractive things about street food was its availability. Take *Pad Thai*, which you could find anywhere day or night, depending on whether you were a well-off day worker or on one of the poorer night shifts. Cheaper versions would be cooked with just a little deep-fried beancurd and sprinkled with some ground dried shrimps to give it some flavour. The more you paid, the more meat or seafood you could request, or you could even get fresh prawns. Today, the grander cooks wrap and serve it in a net of fried egg strands to customers waiting in Mercedes, but in its original adaptable state it was, for a time, virtually the national dish, found everywhere and served in one form or another to everyone.

2 tablespoons vegetable oil

2 garlic cloves, finely chopped

4 raw king or tiger prawns, peeled and de-veined

1 large egg

175g (6oz) *sen lek* noodles (see page 24), soaked and drained

2 tablespoons lemon juice

1¹/₂ tablespoons fish sauce

¹/₂ teaspoon granulated sugar, plus extra to serve

2 tablespoons crushed roasted peanuts

2 tablespoons dried shrimps (see page 19), ground or pounded

¹/₂ teaspoon chilli powder, plus extra to serve

1 tablespoon chopped preserved radish (*chi po*, see page 21)

30g (1oz) fresh beansprouts

2 spring onions, cut into 2.5cm (1in) lengths

to garnish

fresh coriander, coarsely chopped

lemon wedges

1 In a wok or frying pan, heat the oil and fry the garlic until golden brown. Add the prawns and stir well. Break in the egg and stir quickly, cooking for a couple of seconds.

2 Add the soaked noodles and stir well. Stir in the lemon juice, fish sauce, sugar, half the peanuts, half the dried shrimp, the chilli powder, preserved radish, 1 tablespoon of the beansprouts and the spring onions. Keep stirring until the noodles are cooked through – about 3 minutes, then turn on to a serving dish.

3 Arrange the remaining peanuts, dried shrimp and beansprouts over the noodle mixture. To serve, place a little pile of chilli powder and another of sugar on the side of the dish to be mixed in as each diner wishes. Garnish with fresh coriander and lemon wedges.

chicken fried rice with basil leaves
khao pad krapow gai

This is one of those rare Thai dishes that has lost some of its original character on its journey from Thailand to the West. The basil leaves are included for their delicate flavour, and because they need very little cooking, we cut the meat into something like mince to shorten the cooking time. In the West, however, because mince is looked down on, many restaurants tend to use larger slices of meat which results in the basil going limp with the longer cooking time. Decide for yourself – if you want an authentic taste, reduce the cooking time by mincing the meat or cutting it very very finely.

2 tablespoons vegetable oil

2 garlic cloves, finely chopped

2 small fresh red chillies, finely chopped

100g (4oz) minced or very finely chopped chicken

1 tablespoon fish sauce

1/4 teaspoon granulated sugar

1 tablespoon light soy sauce

20 fresh holy basil leaves

225g (8oz) boiled fragrant rice

1 small onion, slivered

1/2 red or green sweet pepper, finely chopped into thin matchsticks

1 In a wok or frying pan, heat the oil until a light haze appears. Add the garlic and fry until golden brown. Stir in the chillies and chicken. Add the fish sauce, sugar and soy sauce and stir-fry over a high heat until the chicken is cooked through.

2 Toss in the basil leaves, followed by the cooked rice and mix gently together. Add the onion and sweet pepper and stir quickly to mix. Turn on to a serving dish.

beef curry with sweet basil
penang nua

2 tablespoons vegetable oil

2 garlic cloves, finely chopped

1 tablespoon red curry paste (see page 25)

175g (6oz) tender beef steak, finely sliced

125ml (4fl oz) coconut cream

1 tablespoon crushed roasted peanuts

20 fresh sweet basil leaves

to garnish

1 long fresh red chilli, finely slivered lengthways

2 kaffir lime leaves, rolled up into a cigarette shape and finely sliced

1 In a wok or frying pan, heat the oil and fry the garlic until it begins to brown. Add the curry paste and stir in well.

2 Add the beef, coconut cream, crushed peanuts and basil leaves, stirring well after each addition. Stir-fry over a high heat until the beef is cooked through.

3 Turn on to a serving dish and garnish with the slivered chilli and kaffir lime leaves.

pork belly with five spices moo pa low

Pork belly with five spices in the foreground and curried rice with chicken, food market, Bangkok.

Street vendors like to serve this dish because it can be prepared in advance and served over several days – unlike many Thai dishes that need to be made at the last minute. It is also thought to be a good, mild accompaniment to hot dishes like curries, so people who have bought the one will often buy this too as a counterbalance.

6 eggs

2 tablespoons vegetable oil

2 large garlic cloves, finely chopped

1 tablespoon finely chopped coriander root

2 tablespoons five-spice powder

675g (1½lb) pork belly, cut into 2.5cm (1in) pieces

1.1 litres (2 pints) chicken stock

2 tablespoons dark soy sauce

3 tablespoons fish sauce

2 tablespoons granulated sugar

to garnish

a few fresh coriander leaves, roughly chopped

1 Hard-boil the eggs, leave to cool, then peel and set aside.

2 In a large saucepan, heat the oil and fry the garlic until golden brown. Stirring constantly, add the coriander root and then the five-spice powder.

3 Add the pork and stir-fry over a high-heat until the meat is thoroughly coated with the spices and cooked through. Pour in the stock and bring to the boil. Stir in the soy sauce, fish sauce and sugar, then add the hard-boiled eggs. Reduce the heat and simmer gently for 30 minutes, skimming off any scum as it forms.

4 Pour into a serving bowl, garnish with fresh coriander leaves and serve.

pork fried with ginger and pineapple moo pad king sapparot

2 tablespoons vegetable oil

2 garlic cloves, finely chopped

225g (8oz) pork fillet, thinly sliced into strips

5 large dried black fungus mushrooms (see page 17), soaked in cold
water for 10 minutes

1 medium onion, roughly chopped

175g (6oz) fresh pineapple chunks

5cm (2in) piece of fresh ginger, peeled and cut into fine matchsticks

2 tablespoons light soy sauce

2 tablespoons vegetable stock

2 spring onions, cut into 2.5cm (1in) lengths

1 long fresh red chilli, sliced diagonally into fine ovals

1/2 teaspoon granulated sugar

a pinch of salt

freshly ground black pepper, to taste

1 In a wok or frying pan, heat the oil and fry the garlic until golden brown.
Add the pork and mushrooms and stir well. Add the remaining ingredients in
turn and stir-fry over a high heat until the pork is cooked through.

2 Season with black pepper and turn on to a serving dish.

for the noodles

1 nest of *ba mee* egg noodles (see page 24)

vegetable oil for deep-frying

for the vegetables

2 tablespoons vegetable oil

1 garlic clove, finely chopped

175g (6oz) boneless chicken breast or thigh, cut into 2.5cm (1in) strips

60g (2oz) bamboo shoots (see page 19), finely sliced

60g (2oz) straw mushrooms, whole or cut in half if large

60g (2oz) baby sweetcorn, cut in half lengthways

60g (2oz) small sweet red or green pepper, seeded and diced

2 spring onions, cut into 2.5cm (1in) lengths, sliced diagonally

1 tablespoon fish sauce

1 teaspoon dark soy sauce

1 teaspoon granulated sugar

$^1/_2$ teaspoon ground white pepper

1 tablespoon cornflour, mixed with 125ml (4fl oz) vegetable stock or cold water to make a thin paste

to garnish

a few fresh coriander leaves

deep-fried noodles with chicken and mixed vegetables go see mee

This is very fast food, popular in bustling city business areas like the area off Silom Road near the Bangkok Bank headquarters. The noodles are deep-fried in advance, the sauce is steaming in its pot – the two ingredients simply have to be brought together, which takes a matter of seconds. It is an ideal party buffet dish, as it leaves the cook free to join in the fun while still proving that he or she has laboured over a hot stove.

1 Separate the strands of egg noodles. Heat the oil to 200°C (400°F) in a deep-fryer and fry the noodles until crisp and golden brown. Remove and drain on kitchen paper, then place on a serving dish and keep warm.

2 In a wok or frying pan, heat the oil until a light haze appears. Add the garlic and fry until golden brown. Add all the remaining ingredients, stirring constantly, finishing with the thin cornflour paste.

3 As soon as the mixture begins to thicken slightly, pour it over the crispy egg noodles. Garnish with fresh coriander and serve immediately.

fried won ton geeow tod

The whole point of fried won ton is that they're served crispy, so while they make good party food, they do have to be cooked at the last minute. When I was a child, there was a Chinese-Thai vendor who used to come down our soi with his won ton already pre-fried. It was strange to us then that no matter how far or for how long he had been wandering around, his won ton were always crispy. Now that I've been in the restaurant business for years, I've learned that they will stay crisp if you keep them in an absolutely air-tight container. You can then serve them cold as long as you make sure the sauce is hot to convince the diner that the won tons have just been cooked. I rather prefer them like that, which is no doubt a memory of childhood.

for the sweet and hot sauces

6 tablespoons rice or white wine vinegar

4 tablespoons granulated sugar

1/2 teaspoon salt

1 small fresh red chilli, finely chopped

1 small fresh green chilli, finely chopped

for the won ton parcels

1 garlic clove, roughly chopped

1 teaspoon roughly chopped coriander root

1 teaspoon whole black peppercorns

1/2 teaspoon salt

1/2 teaspoon granulated sugar

85g (3oz) minced pork

20 won ton pastry sheets (see page 21)

vegetable oil for deep-frying

1 To make the sweet and hot sauces, place the vinegar, sugar and salt in a small saucepan and stir over a low heat until the sugar has dissolved. Allow to cool, then divide between 2 small serving bowls. Stir the chopped chillies into one of the bowls of sauce.

2 To make the won ton filling, pound the garlic, coriander root and peppercorns in a mortar to form a paste. Turn into a mixing bowl and stir in the salt and sugar. Add the minced pork and combine thoroughly with your hands.

3 Lay the pastry squares on a work surface and place a nugget of the filling in the centre of each. Fold each square in half diagonally to make a triangle, brushing the edges with water and pressing lightly to seal.

4 Heat the oil to 200°C (400°F) in a deep-fryer and fry the won ton parcels until golden brown. Drain on kitchen paper and serve immediately with the sweet and hot sauces.

southern salad salad kaek

for the salad

crisp lettuce leaves

1 pink onion, sliced

1/4 English cucumber, cut into very thin slices

60g (2oz) beansprouts

1 medium tomato, cut into wedges

for the sauce

2 tablespoons vegetable oil

1 garlic clove, finely chopped

1 tablespoon red curry paste (see page 25)

60g (2oz) coconut cream

2 tablespoons crushed roasted peanuts

1 teaspoon granulated sugar

3 tablespoons light soy sauce

2 tablespoons lemon juice

3 tablespoons vegetable stock

to garnish

60g (2oz) ready-fried beancurd (see page 19), cut into 2.5cm (1in) cubes

2 medium potatoes, sliced wafer thin and deep-fried until crisp (or a
  packet of potato crisps)

1 Prepare the salad by tossing the ingredients together, and set aside.

2 Heat the oil in a wok or frying pan and fry the garlic until golden brown. Add the curry paste and stir briefly. Pour in the coconut cream and bring to the boil, stirring well. Stir in the crushed peanuts, sugar, soy sauce, lemon juice and vegetable stock. Remove from heat and leave to cool completely.

3 To serve, either pour the sauce over the salad and garnish with beancurd cubes and potato crisps (do not toss the salad as this will be done by the diners), or serve each element separately.

prawns wrapped in beancurd sheet heh guen

for the sweet and sour plum sauce

125ml (4fl oz) rice or white wine vinegar

125ml (4fl oz) granulated sugar

1 teaspoon preserved plum (see page 21), stoned

for the prawns

2 garlic cloves, peeled

2 coriander roots

175g (6oz) raw prawns, peeled and coarsely chopped

30g (1oz) pork fat, finely chopped

ground white pepper, to season

1 egg

4–5 beancurd sheets (see page 19), soaked in cold water for 8–10
  minutes until soft

vegetable oil for deep-frying

1 To make the sauce, place the vinegar and sugar in a heavy-based pan and heat gently to dissolve the sugar. Bring to the boil and boil rapidly to make a thick syrup. Add the plum, breaking it up in the syrup with a metal fork. Pour into a small bowl and leave to cool.

2 To make the filling, pound the garlic with the coriander roots in a mortar. Transfer to a mixing bowl and combine thoroughly with the chopped prawns, pork fat, white pepper and egg.

3 Lay the beancurd sheets on a work surface and divide the filling between each. Roll up to form 'spring roll' shapes about 13–15cm (5–6in) long, tucking in the ends. The beancurd sheets need to be handled carefully as they tend to tear, but you can patch them if necessary. You should finish with about 3 thicknesses of sheet around the prawn filling.

4 Place the rolls in a steamer and steam for 10 minutes, during which time the beancurd will tighten around the filling. Remove from the steamer and leave to cool. The rolls can now be set aside for deep-frying later, or wrapped and stored in the refrigerator for frying the following day. They may also be frozen.

5 To finish, cut each roll into 5–6 rounds or into diagonal pieces. Heat the oil in a deep-fryer to 200°C (400°F) or until a light haze appears, and deep-fry the pieces until golden brown. Remove and drain on kitchen paper. Serve with the sweet and sour plum sauce.

hot fire morning glory
pak boong fi daeng

2 tablespoons vegetable oil

1 garlic clove, finely chopped

4 small fresh red or green chillies, finely chopped

1 tablespoon yellow bean sauce

225g (8oz) morning glory, roughly cut into 5cm (2in) lengths

4 tablespoons vegetable stock

1 tablespoon light soy sauce

1 teaspoon granulated sugar

1 Heat the oil in a wok or frying pan. Add the garlic and chillies and fry until the garlic is golden brown.

2 Add the yellow bean sauce, stir quickly, then add the morning glory, stirring once. Pour in the vegetable stock and simmer gently until the stems of the morning glory start to soften.

3 Season with the soy sauce and sugar, stir once, then turn on to a serving dish.

fried noodles with chicken
gueyteow koua gai

1 tablespoon vegetable oil

1 garlic clove, finely chopped

100g (4oz) boneless chicken breast or thigh, finely sliced

1 egg

1 teaspoon chopped preserved radish (*chi po*, see page 21)

225g (8oz) (wet weight) soaked *sen yai* noodles (see page 24), drained
  and separated

1 tablespoon light soy sauce

a pinch of sugar

1 tablespoon fish sauce

1 large spring onion, chopped

ground white pepper, to taste

to serve
lettuce leaves

to garnish
fresh coriander, coarsely chopped

1 Line a serving dish with roughly torn lettuce leaves and set aside.

2 Heat the oil in a wok or frying pan and fry the garlic until golden brown. Add the chicken and stir-fry over a high heat until the meat is cooked through. Break the egg into the wok or pan and stir quickly. Add the remaining ingredients, one by one, stirring quickly after each addition. Make sure the noodles do not stick to the pan.

3 Turn the mixture on to a serving dish and garnish with fresh coriander.

pork satay moo satay

(serves 4 – see page 14)

So universal is *satay* in Thailand that it amazes people when I say that it used to be a rarity, originally sold only by muslim Malays travelling around the markets and festivals, mainly in the south. Although you did get a large bunch of them, traditional satay only had a tiny curl of meat – just enough for one dip of sauce before you put the whole thing in your mouth. Now they're everywhere and bigger, but not as much of a treat as they were.

for the pork skewers

2 teaspoons coriander seeds

1/2 teaspoon cumin seeds

2 garlic cloves, roughly chopped

2.5cm (1in) piece each of fresh ginger and turmeric, finely chopped

4 small red shallots, finely chopped

1 teaspoon salt

2 tablespoons granulated sugar

2 tablespoons vegetable oil

450g (1lb) lean pork steak, sliced into thin strips 10 x 1cm (4 x 1/2in)

20 bamboo satay sticks

for the satay sauce

2 large dried red chillies, finely chopped

2 garlic cloves, finely chopped

1 stalk of lemon grass, finely chopped

2.5cm (1in) piece of fresh turmeric, finely chopped

2 tablespoons vegetable oil

450ml (3/4 pint) coconut milk

1 tablespoon tamarind water (see page 21)

2 tablespoons granulated sugar

1/2 teaspoon salt

4 tablespoons crushed peanuts

1 First, make the pork skewers. In a mortar, pound together the coriander and cumin seeds, garlic, ginger, turmeric and shallots to make a paste. Stir in the salt, sugar and oil. Turn into a bowl, add the pork strips and combine well to coat the meat thoroughly. Leave to marinate for 1 hour.

2 While the pork is marinating, make the satay sauce. In a mortar, pound together the chillies, garlic, lemon grass and turmeric to form a paste. Heat the oil in a wok or frying pan and stir in the paste. Add the coconut milk, stir well and bring to the boil. Add the tamarind water, sugar, salt and crushed peanuts, stirring between each addition. Simmer for 3 minutes, then pour into a serving bowl.

3 When the pork is marinated, fold each strip of meat in a ripple and pierce through the folds with a satay stick, as if sewing.

4 Place the sticks under a hot grill or on a barbecue, turning from time to time, until cooked through. Serve with the satay sauce.

green chicken curry
gaeng kiow wan gai

Outside Thailand, this is the most popular of all the Thai curries. I'd be hard pressed to say why, but I must admit it's my favourite too. Perhaps because it was one of my mother's specialities and my dad was always asking for it.

125ml (4fl oz) coconut cream

2 tablespoons vegetable oil

1 garlic clove, finely chopped

1 tablespoon green curry paste (see page 25)

2 tablespoons fish sauce

1 teaspoon granulated sugar

175g (6oz) chicken breast or thigh, cut into thin strips

100ml (3¹/₂ fl oz) chicken stock

2 kaffir lime leaves, chopped

3 small green aubergines (see page 15), quartered

15 fresh holy basil leaves

1 In a small pan, gently heat the coconut cream but do not boil. Set aside.

2 Heat the oil in a wok or frying pan, add the chopped garlic and fry until golden brown. Add the curry paste and stir-fry for a few seconds. Add the warmed coconut cream and stir until it curdles and thickens in the oil. Stir in the fish sauce and sugar. Add the chicken strips and turn in the mixture until the meat becomes opaque.

3 Pour in the stock and simmer gently for 3–4 minutes, stirring occasionally.

4 Add the lime leaves, then stir in the aubergines and basil leaves. Cook for 1 minute more, then turn on to a serving dish.

steamed crab meat
bu ja

Another street dish that is quick to prepare for busy city workers, the crab is already steamed in its shell and ready to eat.

3 garlic cloves, skinned

3 coriander roots

100g (4oz) crab meat

100g (4oz) minced pork

1 egg

1 tablespoon fish sauce

1 tablespoon light soy sauce

¹/₂ teaspoon granulated sugar

3–4 crab shells or small ramekins, to serve

to garnish

8 fine slivers fresh red chilli

8 fine slivers fresh green chilli

fresh coriander leaves

1 Pound the garlic with the coriander roots in a mortar to form a paste. Transfer to a mixing bowl and combine with all the remaining ingredients, except the garnishes. Divide the mixture between the crab shells or ramekins and place in a steamer. Steam for 15 minutes.

2 Remove from the steamer and garnish with the slivers of red and green chilli and the fresh coriander leaves.

gold bags tung tong

for the dipping sauce
4 tablespoons granulated sugar
4 tablespoons rice or white vinegar
1/2 teaspoon salt
1 small fresh red chilli, cut into fine rings
1 small fresh green chilli, cut into fine rings

for the gold bags
100g (4oz) minced pork
2 water chestnuts (see page 21), chopped
1 garlic clove, very finely chopped
ground white pepper, to season
12 small won ton wrappers (see page 21), about 7.5 x 7.5cm (3 x 3in)
vegetable oil for deep-frying

1 First make the dipping sauce. In a small saucepan, dissolve the sugar in the vinegar over a low heat. Bring to the boil and boil rapidly, stirring, to give a pale golden syrup. Stir in the salt and sliced chillies and pour into a small bowl. (The sauce will thicken slightly as it cools.)

2 To make the filling, place the pork, water chestnuts, garlic and a sprinkling of pepper in a mixing bowl and combine well.

3 Lay the won ton wrappers on a work surface and place 1 teaspoon of the filling in the middle of each. Gather up the 4 corners of each with your fingertips and pinch them together to form a small bag.

4 To cook, heat the oil in a deep-fryer to 200°C (400°F) or until a light haze appears and fry the won ton bags until crisp and deep golden brown. Drain on kitchen paper and serve with the dipping sauce.

rice soup khaotom

2 tablespoons vegetable oil
1 garlic clove, coarsely chopped
850ml (1 1/2 pints) chicken stock
225g (8oz) boiled fragrant rice
60g (2oz) boneless chicken breast or thigh, thinly sliced
1/2 teaspoon chopped preserved vegetables (tang *chi*, see page 21)
1 tablespoon fish sauce
1 tablespoon soy sauce
1/2 teaspoon granulated sugar
2.5cm (1in) piece of fresh ginger, finely chopped
1/2 teaspoon ground white pepper

to garnish
1 spring onion, finely sliced
a few fresh coriander leaves

1 In a small pan, heat the oil and fry the garlic until golden brown. Set aside to infuse, reserving both the oil and the garlic.

2 Heat the stock in a large pan, add the cooked rice and slices of chicken and bring to the boil.

3 Stir in all the remaining ingredients and simmer gently for about 30 seconds, or until the chicken is cooked through.

4 Pour into a serving bowl and drizzle over a little of the reserved garlic oil. Garnish with finely sliced spring onion and fresh coriander leaves.

pork fried with red curry paste and long beans pad prik king moo

2 tablespoons vegetable oil

1 tablespoon red curry paste (see page 25)

275g (10oz) pork fillet, finely sliced

175g (6oz) long beans (see page 17), cut into 5cm (2in) lengths

2 tablespoons fish sauce

1 teaspoon granulated sugar

1 Heat the oil in a wok or frying pan, add the red curry paste and stir well. Add the pork and stir-fry for a minute or two until the meat is cooked through.

2 Add the beans, fish sauce and sugar, stir thoroughly, then transfer to a serving dish.

steamed sticky rice with banana khao tom pad

This is handy travelling food because everything is wrapped in banana leaves out of which the rice can be easily eaten – which is why you always find vendors with trays of them at long-distance bus terminals and train stations, or even walking down the corridors of the carriages themselves. Good for picnics when you don't want to haul plates and knives round.

225g (8oz) sticky rice (see page 22), soaked for 3–4 hours

500ml (18fl oz) coconut milk

1/2 teaspoon salt

4 tablespoons granulated sugar

5 small bananas, each about 10cm (4in) long, peeled and cut in half
  lengthways

banana leaves (see page 15) or tin foil, to serve

1 Drain the sticky rice and place it in a saucepan with the coconut milk. Bring up to simmering point, stirring constantly until the rice has just absorbed the liquid – about 5–10 minutes. At this point, the rice will be half-cooked. Stir in the salt and sugar, then remove from the heat and leave to cool.

2 Make 10 rectangles about 25 x 20cm (10 x 8in) out of banana leaves or tin foil. Place 2 tablespoons half-cooked rice on each rectangle, flatten gently, then place a half-length of banana on top of each. Wrap up tightly by folding over first the long then the short sides.

3 Place folded-side down in the upper compartment of a steamer and steam for 30 minutes. Serve in the leaf or foil wrapping, hot or cold.

Barbecued pork.

sticky rice with mango khao niew mamuang

This is easily the most popular Thai dessert, both with Thais who are great mango connoisseurs and with Westerners, probably because it isn't as sweet as other Thai *khanom*, which take a little getting used to. Sweet juicy mango served with firm sticky rice and slightly salty coconut cream really is the perfectly balanced *yin* and *yang* combination. And if you can get to Khun Pa Ni Chiapchalaart's street shop in Bangkok, you can sample this treat at its best.

250ml (9fl oz) coconut milk

2 tablespoons granulated sugar

1/2 teaspoon salt

275g (10oz) sticky rice (see page 22), cooked and still warm

4 ripe mangoes

2 tablespoons coconut cream

1 Combine the coconut milk and sugar in a small saucepan and heat gently, stirring all the time, until the sugar has dissolved. Do not allow to boil.

2 Stir in the salt and warm, cooked sticky rice and set aside.

3 Peel the mangoes and cut off the 2 outer 'cheeks' of each fruit, as close to the centre stone as possible. Discard the stone. Slice each piece of fruit into 4 lengths.

4 Place a mound of sticky rice in the centre of a serving dish and arrange the slices of mango around it. Pour the coconut cream over the sticky rice and serve warm or cold.

When you leave the city, you can sometimes feel lost for somewhere to eat. No matter, there is a solution to hand. In Thailand, street food sellers can always be found near any public building, ready to supply workers and visitors with a meal. You can always combine a visit to a temple with lunch or dinner, they adorn many city streets and are found in every village. There are generally fruit sellers nearby (like the one on the left), to provide gifts of food that worshippers might want to present to the monks to gain merit – or simply to refresh themselves on a hot day.

around bangkok

fish cakes with fresh pickle
tod man pla

(serves 4–6 – see page 14)

I tend to judge chefs by how well or badly they make this dish. The cakes have to be tender but not too soft – I know it sounds unappetising, but the word 'rubbery' springs to mind. The mixture should be kneaded gently but firmly, like a first class masseuse working on a tired muscle. Because street-sellers generally specialise in one dish and therefore get a lot of practise at it, I usually have this whenever I see it.

for the fresh pickle

125ml (4fl oz) rice or white wine vinegar

2 tablespoons granulated sugar

5cm (2in) piece of English cucumber, unpeeled

1 small carrot

3 shallots, finely sliced

1 medium fresh red chilli, finely sliced

1 tablespoon crushed roasted peanuts, to serve

for the fish cakes

5 dried red chillies, halved and de-seeded

1 shallot, finely sliced

2 garlic cloves, peeled

2 coriander roots, roughly chopped

1 tablespoon finely chopped galangal (see page 17)

6 kaffir lime leaves, finely chopped

1/2 teaspoon salt

450g (1lb) white fish fillet (cod, coley, haddock or monkfish), minced for
 a few seconds in a food processor

1 tablespoon fish sauce

60g (2oz) long beans (see page 17) or French beans, sliced very finely

vegetable oil for deep-frying

1 To make the pickle, place the vinegar and sugar in a small saucepan and heat gently until the sugar dissolves. Bring to the boil and boil rapidly for 6–7 minutes until a thin syrup is formed. Pour into a bowl and leave to cool.

2 Quarter the cucumber lengthways, then slice finely across. Halve the carrot lengthways and slice finely across. Add the cucumber, carrot, shallots and chilli to the cold syrup and mix thoroughly. Set aside.

3 To make the fishcakes, pound the chillies, shallot, garlic, coriander roots, galangal, kaffir lime leaves and salt in a mortar to form a paste. Place the minced fish in a mixing bowl, add the paste and combine thoroughly with your fingers. Mix in the fish sauce and finely sliced green beans and knead firmly together. Divide into 20 balls, then form into flat cakes about 5cm (2in) across and 1cm (1/2in) thick.

4 Heat the oil in a deep-fryer to 200°C (400°F) and deep-fry the cakes until golden brown, about 2–3 minutes. Drain on kitchen paper then arrange on a serving platter.

5 Sprinkle the crushed peanuts over the pickle and serve with the hot fish cakes.

chicken with holy basil
gai pad krapow

This dish can be prepared with chicken or beef.

2 tablespoons vegetable oil

2 garlic cloves, finely chopped

2 small fresh red or green chillies, finely chopped

175g (6oz) minced chicken

1 medium onion, halved and roughly sliced

2 tablespoons fish sauce

1 tablespoon soy sauce

1 teaspoon granulated sugar

20 fresh holy basil leaves

1 In a wok or frying pan, heat the oil and fry the garlic and chillies, stirring well, until the garlic begins to brown.

2 Add the minced chicken and stir-fry over a high heat, breaking apart the meat and mixing in the garlic and chilli.

3 Add all the remaining ingredients to the pan and continue to stir-fry until the chicken is cooked through. Turn on to a dish and serve.

rice noodles with coconut
meegrat ti

2 small shallots, peeled

8 black peppercorns

1 large fresh red chilli, roughly chopped

1/2 teaspoon salt

6 tablespoons coconut cream

3 tablespoons vegetable stock or water

1 teaspoon granulated sugar

1/2 teaspoon chilli powder

2 tablespoons light soy sauce

100g (4oz) dry *sen mee* noodles (see page 24), soaked in water for about 20 minutes

60g (2oz) ready-fried beancurd (see page 19), sliced into thin squares

100g (4oz) beansprouts

1 spring onion, finely chopped

to garnish
a few fresh coriander leaves

1 Pound the shallots, peppercorns, chilli and salt in a mortar to form a paste.

2 Warm the coconut cream in a saucepan or wok, but do not let it boil. Stir in the vegetable stock or water, the sugar, chilli powder and soy sauce. Add the paste from the mortar, stirring continuously, until all the ingredients are blended together.

3 Strain the noodles and add to the sauce. Simmer gently until almost cooked through, then add the beancurd, beansprouts and spring onion. Mix quickly, turn on to a serving dish and garnish with fresh coriander leaves. Serve hot or cold.

chicken rice khao man gai

(serves 4–6 – see page 14)

This dish is originally from Hunan Island in southern China. The Hunanese were very poor and emigration was common. The travellers took with them a simple, cheap cuisine of which this is the most famous example. It is now found all over southeast Asia, I suspect because anyone starting in the street food business doesn't need much capital outlay to start producing it. Anyway, like lots of simple peasant dishes, it is delicious, easy to find and best of all for first time visitors to Asia, not too hot.

for the chicken

1 medium chicken, about 1.5kg (3lb 5oz)

6 garlic cloves, lightly crushed

1/2 teaspoon salt

450g (1lb) fragrant rice, rinsed

for the sauce

1/2 tablespoon yellow bean sauce

5cm (2in) piece of fresh ginger, finely chopped

3 garlic cloves, finely chopped

5 small fresh red or green chillies, finely chopped

1 teaspoon dark soy sauce

2 tablespoons light soy sauce

2 tablespoons rice or white wine vinegar

1 tablespoon granulated sugar

for the accompaniment

1/2 English cucumber, sliced into rings

a large handful of fresh coriander leaves, roughly chopped

2 spring onions, finely chopped

freshly ground black pepper

1 Place the chicken in a large saucepan and just cover with cold water. Remove the chicken and set aside. Add 4 of the garlic cloves and the salt to the pan and bring to the boil. Place the chicken in the boiling water, cover with a lid and boil for 20 minutes. Lower the heat and simmer for a further 10 minutes. Remove the chicken and place on a rack to drain completely, reserving the water or stock.

2 Place the rice in a medium pan and add enough of the chicken stock so that the liquid is 2.5cm (1in) above the level of the rice. Add the 2 remaining garlic cloves, cover with a lid and bring to the boil. Remove the lid, stir once, then replace the lid and leave to simmer very gently for 20 minutes without lifting the lid again. After this time, the rice should have absorbed all the liquid and be fluffy, with each grain separate. Remove from the heat, covered, and set aside.

3 Make the sauce. In a small bowl, mix together all the ingredients and set aside.

4 Prepare a small plate of sliced cucumber and chopped coriander leaves and set aside. Carefully carve the chicken into thin slices, retaining any skin but discarding the bones. Set aside.

5 Reheat the remaining stock and pour into individual soup bowls. Garnish with the finely chopped spring onions and a little black pepper and put on the table along with the bowl of hot sauce and the plate of cucumber and coriander. Take a plate for each diner, place a good helping of rice on each and arrange the slices of chicken on top. To serve, everyone eats their own rice and chicken and sips their own soup – or pours a little soup over their rice if they wish – while they share the sauce and cucumber.

barbecued pork with rice khao moo deang

(serves 6 – see page 14)

Another dish of Chinese origin, simple, not too spicy and easy to find – especially in pig-breeding areas like Nakhon Pathom, where this dish is a great speciality in the street food area around the giant temple (*chedi*).

for the barbecued pork
4 tablespoons tomato purée
2 tablespoons dark soy sauce
4 tablespoons light soy sauce
4 tablespoons granulated sugar
1kg (2lb 3oz) pork belly strips
450g (1lb) fragrant rice, rinsed and drained

for the chilli and vinegar sauce
4 tablespoons rice or white wine vinegar
1 small fresh red chilli, cut into thin rounds

for the salty sauce
450ml (³/4 pint) pork stock
2 tablespoons light soy sauce
3 tablespoons granulated sugar
2 tablespoons fish sauce
1 teaspoon rice flour

to garnish
1/4 English cucumber, thinly sliced
4 spring onions, cut into 2.5cm (1in) lengths
6 hard-boiled eggs, peeled and cut into quarters
a few fresh coriander leaves, roughly chopped

1 Prepare the marinade by combining the tomato purée, soy sauces and sugar in a large bowl. Add the pork belly strips and stir well to coat evenly in the sauce. Leave to marinate for 1 hour.

2 Cook the rice, drain and set aside.

3 Place the marinated pork belly strips on a barbecue or under a preheated grill, turning them from time to time until cooked through.

4 While the pork is cooking, make the sauces. For the chilli and vinegar sauce, combine the ingredients in a small bowl and set aside. For the salty sauce, heat the stock in a saucepan, add all the ingredients except the rice flour and stir well. Bring to the boil and simmer for 1 minute. Sprinkle the rice flour over the liquid and whisk gently until the sauce thickens.

5 Cut the pork into very thin slices. (In the West, it is often cut too thickly, whereas in Asia it is always cut as thinly as sliced ham.)

6 Put a heap of rice on each serving plate and top with thin slices of barbecued pork. Pour over a good helping of the salty sauce. Garnish each plate with sliced cucumber, 1 or 2 short lengths of spring onion , coriander and a quartered hard-boiled egg. Serve with the chilli and vinegar sauce.

fried river noodles with beef and dark soy pad si yew

1 tablespoon vegetable oil

2 garlic cloves, finely chopped

100g (4oz) tender beef steak, finely sliced

1 egg

225g (8oz) (wet weight) soaked *sen yai* noodles (see page 24), drained

60g (2oz) broccoli, cut into small florets

1/2 teaspoon dark soy sauce

1 tablespoon light soy sauce

a pinch of sugar

2 tablespoons fish sauce

ground white pepper, to taste

chilli powder, to season (optional)

1 In a wok or frying pan, heat the oil and fry the garlic until golden brown. Add the beef and stir-fry over a high heat to seal the juices. Break the egg into the pan and stir quickly until lightly set.

2 Add the noodles to the pan, tossing well to prevent them from sticking, then add the broccoli and stir again. Stir in the soy sauces, sugar and fish sauce, then turn on to a serving dish. Season with a sprinkling of ground white pepper and chilli powder, if using.

grilled fish with coriander and garlic pla pow

6 coriander roots

3 large garlic cloves, peeled

ground white pepper, to taste

1 medium mackerel or whiting, cleaned and patted dry inside and out

1 large banana leaf (see page 15) or tin foil

to garnish

lettuce leaves

1 Pound the coriander roots and garlic together in a mortar to form a paste, or blend in a food processor. Season the mixture with a generous shaking of ground white pepper.

2 Put this paste inside the cavity of the cleaned fish, then wrap the fish in a banana leaf or tin foil. If using a banana leaf, simply roll the wide leaf around the stuffed fish, fold the ends over and secure with cocktail sticks. Preheat the grill to medium.

3 Grill the wrapped fish for about 6–8 minutes on each side.

4 To serve, simply unwrap the fish and place on a bed of lettuce.

pork and fish ball noodles
gueyteow haeng moo

This is another quick dish – the street sellers usually ride on an adapted vehicle which is the back half of a bicycle with a sort of wheeled box at the front. The box contains a pot of water, constantly on the boil, and a glass-fronted display case with noodles and all the other ingredients and spices they need. All you have to do is flag the seller down and point. Anything you indicate will be put into a large strainer, which is dipped in the water for a few seconds and then turned into a bowl. Effectively you are the chef, so you have no one to blame except yourself if it doesn't taste good.

2 tablespoons vegetable oil

2 garlic cloves, finely chopped

1 teaspoon chopped preserved vegetables (*tang chi*, see page 21)

1 tablespoon fish sauce

1 tablespoon light soy sauce

1/2 teaspoon granulated sugar

30g (1oz) beansprouts

225g (8oz) *sen lek* noodles (see page 24), soaked, drained and separated

3 pork balls (see page 21)

3 fish balls (see page 19)

4 slices fish cake (see page 19)

4 slices cold boiled pork

1 tablespoon crushed roasted peanuts

1 sprig of fresh coriander, coarsely chopped

1 In a wok or frying pan, heat the oil and fry the garlic until golden brown. Set aside to infuse, reserving the oil and garlic.

2 Put the preserved radish, fish sauce, soy sauce and sugar into a deep serving bowl, mix quickly and set aside.

3 Bring a large pan of water to the boil. Using a wire-meshed ladle or a small coarse sieve with a handle, dip the beansprouts into the boiling water for 3 seconds to just heat through. Turn the drained beansprouts into the serving bowl, reserving the boiling water.

4 Dip the noodles into the boiling water in the same way – again, only for a few seconds – shaking them slightly to separate the strands. Drain and add to the serving bowl. Pour over 1 tablespoon of the reserved oil and garlic (this will help to separate the noodles, as well as adding flavour).

5 In turn, dip the pork balls, fish balls and fish cake slices into the boiling water, heating them through completely before adding them to the serving bowl. Arrange the slices of cold pork (without heating them) over the noodles. To serve, sprinkle the dish with crushed peanuts and fresh coriander and mix quickly together. To turn this dish into noodle soup, simply pour on 450ml (3/4 pint) hot stock before garnishing with the peanuts and coriander.

mussels in batter with egg hoy tohd

In Thailand, this is also made with oysters, which are just as cheap as mussels. This makes it popular with street sellers because it doesn't cost them much to start up in business. The consequence is that you find it everywhere – the public like it too, mainly because it is very light and so makes a good late night snack after a show or club.

for the chilli-vinegar sauce

3 tablespoons rice or white wine vinegar

2 small fresh chillies, finely sliced into rings

1/2 teaspoon granulated sugar

for the batter

3 tablespoons rice flour

3 tablespoons plain (wheat) flour

a pinch of salt

1 egg

200ml (7fl oz) water

for the mussels

175g (6oz) mussels, soaked, cleaned, de-bearded and shelled

2 tablespoons vegetable oil, plus extra if necessary

1 egg

a handful of beansprouts

1 spring onion, coarsely chopped

ground white pepper, to taste

1 tablespoon light soy sauce

1 tablespoon fish sauce

1 teaspoon granulated sugar

to garnish

a few fresh coriander leaves

1 In a small bowl, mix all the ingredients for the chilli-vinegar sauce together and set aside.

2 To make the batter, combine the flours and salt in a bowl. Make a well in the centre, break in the egg and add the water. Whisk thoroughly together, making sure there are no lumps – the mixture should have the consistency of thick cream.

3 Add the shelled mussels to the batter, coat thoroughly and set aside.

4 In a large wok or frying pan, heat the oil, add the mussel and batter mixture and tilt the pan from side to side to spread the mixture evenly over the surface. Cook the 'pancake' for 1–2 minutes, then flip over and cook the other side briefly until it is set. Divide the pancake into 5 or 6 portions with a spatula and a wooden spoon. Lower the heat and break the second egg into the pan. Quickly cook the pancake pieces in the egg, adding a little more oil if necessary.

5 Stir in the beansprouts and spring onion, then season with a sprinkling of white pepper. Add the soy sauce, fish sauce and sugar, turning the pancake pieces over quickly to absorb the liquid. Place on a warm serving dish and garnish with fresh coriander. Serve with the chilli-vinegar sauce.

prawns with lemon grass pla gung

2 tablespoons lemon juice

2 tablespoons fish sauce

1/2 teaspoon chilli powder

1 teaspoon granulated sugar

2 tablespoons fish stock or water

5–6 large raw prawns, shelled and de-veined

1 kaffir lime leaf, finely chopped

1 shallot, coarsely chopped

1 stalk lemon grass, finely chopped

1/2 small onion, slivered

1 spring onion, cut into 2.5cm (1in) pieces

to serve
lettuce leaves and fresh parsley sprigs

1   Line a small serving plate with lettuce leaves and sprigs of parsley and set aside.

2   Place the lemon juice, fish sauce, chilli powder, sugar and stock in a small wok or frying pan and boil rapidly for about 1 minute, stirring all the time until considerably reduced. Add the shelled prawns and cook quickly until the prawns are opaque. Add all the remaining ingredients, stir once, remove from the heat and transfer to the prepared serving plate. Serve immediately.

curried noodles gueyteow kak

100g (4oz) lean beef steak, cut into 2.5cm (1in) cubes

1 hard-boiled egg, peeled

3 tablespoons vegetable oil

1 block ready-fried beancurd (see page 19), finely sliced

1 shallot, finely chopped

1 garlic clove, finely chopped

2 teaspoons red curry paste (see page 25)

4 tablespoons coconut milk

1 teaspoon curry powder

1 tablespoon fish sauce

1 teaspoon granulated sugar

60g (2oz) dry *sen lek* noodles (see page 24), soaked, drained
  and separated

1 tablespoon crushed roasted peanuts

to garnish

a few fresh coriander leaves

1 Put the beef in a small pan and cover with water. Bring to the boil, then simmer gently for 10–15 minutes. Cut the egg into quarters and set aside. Heat a pan of water ready for the noodles.

2 In a small frying pan, heat 1 tablespoon oil and fry the sliced beancurd until slightly crisp. Drain and set aside, reserving the oil in the pan.

3 Reheat the oil (adding a little more, if necessary) and fry the shallot until dark golden brown and crisp. Set aside in the pan.

4 In a wok or large frying pan, heat 2 tablespoons oil, add the garlic and fry until golden brown. Stir in the curry paste and cook for a few seconds, then pour in the coconut milk and heat through. Do not allow to boil.

5 With a slotted spoon or strainer, remove the beef from its pan (reserving the cooking liquid) and add to the curried sauce. Stir to make sure each piece is coated in the sauce. Add 450ml (3/4 pint) of the cooking liquid (make up the amount with cold water if necessary), then add the curry powder, fish sauce and sugar. Stir everything together and simmer gently for about 5 minutes.

6 Bring the water for the noodles to the boil. Put the noodles in a sieve or strainer with a handle and dip them into the boiling water for 2–3 seconds, or until heated through. Drain and divide between 2 serving bowls. Arrange the quartered egg on top of each bowl of noodles. Stir the crushed peanuts into the beef curry soup and pour over the noodles. Garnish with the reserved fried beancurd, fried shallot with a little of its cooking oil and the fresh coriander.

Man cooking a late-night supper at the night market.

fried prawns with chilli and lime leaf
chu chee gung

2 tablespoons vegetable oil

2 garlic cloves, finely chopped

1 tablespoon red curry paste (see page 25)

2 tablespoons fish stock or water

6–8 raw king or tiger prawns, shelled and de-veined

2 tablespoons fish sauce

1 tablespoon granulated sugar

1 tablespoon lemon juice

2 kaffir lime leaves, finely chopped

1 long fresh red chilli, finely slivered

1 Heat the oil in a wok or frying pan, add the garlic and fry until golden brown. Stir in the curry paste and cook together for a few seconds. Add the stock and mix thoroughly. Toss in the prawns and stir-fry for a few seconds until opaque.

2 Add the fish sauce, sugar, lemon juice, lime leaves and chilli, stirring after each addition. Cook together for 2–3 seconds, then turn on to a serving dish. This dish should be quite dry.

curried chicken steamed in banana leaf haw muk

If possible, you should use banana leaves to make the little cups in which the curried chicken is steamed. If you can't find any, use small heatproof bowls or ramekins the size of a teacup instead.

4 banana leaves (see page 15) or large ramekins

2 heaped tablespoons chopped Chinese cabbage

175g (6oz) boneless chicken breast or thigh, cut into thin slices

2 teaspoons red curry paste (see page 25)

10 fresh holy basil leaves, finely chopped

3 kaffir lime leaves, finely chopped

1 egg

2 tablespoons thick coconut cream

1 tablespoon fish sauce

to garnish

2 tablespoons thick coconut milk

1 long fresh red chilli, shredded

3 kaffir lime leaves, shredded

1 First make the banana leaf cups. Cut the banana leaves into 12.5cm (5in) squares – you will need 2 squares for each cup. Place 2 squares, 1 on top of the other on a work surface. Place a 10cm (4in) bowl upside-down on top and cut around the bowl to give 2 circles of banana leaf. Place the circles dull sides facing eachother. Make a 1cm (1/2in) tuck about 4cm (11/2in) deep at any point on the circumference and staple together. Repeat this at the opposite point. You will now have a slightly opened, squared-off cup.

2 Place a little Chinese cabbage in the bottom of each banana leaf cup and set aside.

3 Place the chicken strips, red curry paste, basil leaves, chopped lime leaves, egg, coconut milk and fish sauce in a bowl and combine well together.

4 Divide the mixture between the banana leaf cups, placing it on top of the chopped cabbage. Drizzle with a little coconut milk and sprinkle with red chilli to garnish.

5 Place the cups in a hot steamer and cook for 20 minutes. Remove and serve immediately.

fried taro pooak tod

Obviously popular with vegetarians, this could also be made with sweet potato.

for the taro

1 egg

150ml (¹/₄ pint) coconut milk

3 tablespoons plain flour

¹/₂ teaspoon salt

1 tablespoon granulated sugar

1 tablespoon sesame seeds

275g (10oz) taro (see page 18), peeled and chopped into small chips

vegetable oil for deep-frying

for the sauce

4 tablespoons granulated sugar

5 tablespoons rice or white wine vinegar

¹/₂ teaspoon salt

¹/₂ teaspoon chilli powder

2 tablespoons crushed roasted peanuts

1 For the taro, combine the egg, coconut milk, flour, salt, sugar and sesame seeds in a mixing bowl and whisk together to form a smooth batter. Add the taro chips, turning them well in the mixture until evenly coated. Set aside.

2 To make the sauce, place the sugar and vinegar in a small saucepan and heat gently stiring until the sugar has dissolved. Bring to the boil and boil rapidly until the mixture thickens. Stir in the salt and chilli powder. Remove from the heat and stir in the crushed peanuts. Pour into a serving bowl.

3 Heat the oil in a deep-fryer to 200°C (400°F) and deep-fry the battered chips until golden brown. Drain on kitchen paper and place on a serving dish. Serve with the sauce.

curried rice and chicken with fresh pickle (adjahd) khao mok gai

(serves 4–6 – see page 14)

This seems to have come north with Muslims from the South, which means it is probably Malay in origin.

for the chicken

1 medium chicken, weighing about 1.3–1.6kg (3–3¹/₂lb)

3 tablespoons vegetable oil

4 large garlic cloves, finely chopped

450g (1lb) fragrant rice, rinsed and drained

2 teaspoons each of curry powder and salt

500ml (18fl oz) chicken stock

for the fresh pickle

4 tablespoons rice or white wine vinegar

2 teaspoons granulated sugar

¹/₂ teaspoon salt

7.5cm (3in) piece of English cucumber

2 small shallots, finely chopped

2–3 small fresh red chillies, thinly sliced

1 Halve the chicken, then chop each half into 3 equal pieces.

2 In a wok or frying pan, heat the oil and fry the garlic until golden brown. Stir in the rice, then add the curry powder and salt. Add the chicken pieces and stir well.

3 Either transfer the mixture to an electric rice-steamer, add the stock, cover and cook for 20 minutes, or put the mixture in a heatproof bowl, add the stock and place in the top part of a steamer over boiling water and steam for 30 minutes.

4 While the chicken is steaming, make the pickle. Warm the vinegar, sugar and salt in a small pan, stirring until the sugar has dissolved. Remove from the heat. Cut the cucumber in half lengthways, then cut it in half again and slice very finely. Add to the sauce with the chopped shallots and chillies. Pour into a serving bowl and serve with the steamed chicken.

gold threads
foy tong

(serves 4–6 – see page 14)

This dish is often served at birthday parties or prepared as an offering to monks on special anniversary days. The look of the dish satisfies two of our desires – it is gold, a propitious colour, and it has long threads indicating a long life. As a consequence, you'll find Foy Tong makers at most street food markets, especially if the market is near a monastery. To make the threads, you will need a special piece of equipment, made by cleaning a tin can and piercing the base with 6 small holes through which liquid can be streamed.

10 jasmine flowers
400ml (14fl oz) water
10 eggs
1 tablespoon vegetable oil
900g (2lb) granulated sugar

1 Sprinkle the jasmine flowers over the water and leave to infuse for 1 hour (see page 19).

2 Separate the egg yolks and reserve the whites. Whisk the yolks in a large bowl until thick and creamy, add the egg whites and oil and whisk to combine.

3 Remove the jasmine flowers from the perfumed water and discard. Pour the water into a large saucepan and add the sugar. Heat gently, stirring to dissolve the sugar, then boil rapidly to form a thin syrup.

4 To make the threads, fill your homemade strainer with the egg mixture and drizzle it in thin streams into the simmering sugar syrup, moving it in a circular motion to form nests of threads. Cook for 1 minute or until golden brown, then remove with a skewer and place on a metal tray to cool.

bananas in thick syrup
kruay chu'am

(serves 4–6 – see page 14)

225g (8oz) granulated sugar
225ml (8fl oz) water
4 large bananas
125ml (4fl oz) coconut milk
1/4 teaspoon salt

1 Place the sugar and water in a heavy-based saucepan and heat gently, stirring until all the sugar has dissolved, the bring to the boil.

2 Peel the bananas and cut into 5cm (2in) pieces. Drop into the saucepan of boiling syrup, then lower the heat and cook gently until the bananas are bright and clear and the sugar syrup forms threads when lifted with a wooden spoon. Remove any scum as it forms.

3 Serve with coconut milk, seasoned with salt to balance the sweetness.

coconut custard sankaya

225g (8oz) granulated sugar

250ml (9fl oz) thick coconut milk

1 teaspoon rosewater

1/2 teaspoon salt

3 eggs, lightly beaten (use whites only, if you have some to use up)

1 Place the sugar and coconut milk in a large pan and heat gently, stirring until the sugar has dissolved. Stir in the rosewater and salt. Add the beaten eggs (or egg whites) and fold in carefully.

2 Pour the resulting custard into a heatproof bowl or metal baking tray. Place in the top of a preheated steamer and cook for 30 minutes, or until set. Cut into small squares 2.5– 4cm (1–1¹/₂in).

jackfruit seeds met kanoon

(serves 4–6 – see page 14)

These are little balls of sweetened bean paste and egg that are moulded to look like jackfruit. Noon means something like 'help and support', so this dish is aptly served at weddings.

225g (8oz) split moong beans (see page 20)

175g (6oz) desiccated coconut

225g (8oz) granulated sugar

350ml (12fl oz) water

2 egg yolks, beaten

1 Rinse the moong beans, place in a small saucepan and cover with 4cm (1¹/₂in) water. Cook gently for 30–45 minutes, or until completely soft.

2 Drain off any excess water and mash thoroughly. Add the desiccated coconut and mix together to form a firm paste. Turn onto a work surface and divide into 20 pieces, each about the size of a small walnut. Shape into small 'eggs'. Set aside.

3 Place the sugar and water in a large saucepan and heat gently, stirring until the sugar has dissolved. Bring to the boil and boil rapidly to form a thin syrup the consistency of runny honey. Dip the 'eggs' in beaten egg yolk and drop into the syrup for a few seconds, or until set. Remove with a small strainer or slotted spoon and set on a wire rack to cool. Serve as sweets.

baked moong bean and coconut custard kanom maw geang

(serves 6 – see page 14)

Phetchaburi is the 'sweet tooth' town. Its surrounding sugar palms make it the centre of the Thai confectionery trade and lots of people make the short car journey to and from Bangkok at weekends and holidays to stock up with puddings and sweets. It has its own street food rags-to-riches story with a woman called Mer Kim Li, who started making puddings like this dish which she sold by the main road leading into the town. Soon her little trays of custard were famous and became the cause of special trips to Phetchaburi by eager Bangkokians. She went on to run a roadside shop, then a restaurant and eventually a chain of them – all from something made out of a handful of beans!

400g (14oz) split moong beans (see page 20)
450ml (³/₄ pint) coconut cream
3 eggs, lightly beaten
450g (1lb) granulated sugar
¹/₂ teaspoon salt
2 tablespoons vegetable oil
4 shallots, finely sliced

Night stall selling sweet noodles, Ayutthaya.

1 Rinse the moong beans in cold water. Place in a saucepan and cover with about 5cm (2in) water. Cook gently for 30–45 minutes or until the beans are completely soft.

2 Pre-heat the oven to 180°C/350°F/gas mark 4. Drain off any excess water and mash the beans to a smooth paste. Stir in the coconut cream, eggs, sugar and salt. Pour the mixture into a shallow, greased baking tin, 23 x 23 x 5cm (9 x 9 x 2in), and bake in a medium oven for about 1 hour, or until golden brown on top and quite firm when pressed lightly.

3 While the pudding is baking, heat the oil in a pan and fry the sliced shallots until dark golden brown. Drain on kitchen paper and set aside.

4 Just before you take the pudding out of the oven, preheat the grill. When the pudding is baked, set it under the grill for about 5 minutes to crisp up the top. Leave to cool in the tin.

5 To serve, sprinkle with the fried shallots, then cut into small squares 2.5– 4cm (1–1¹/₂in).

A trip to the seaside for a group of Thai friends is always an excuse for a feast. Every popular beach area has its parade of itinerant food sellers selling fish and seafood specialities such as grilled squid, prawns in batter and steamed mussels. Many walk up and down the beach with their *hahps*, others congregate together to form beachside restaurants. Many visitors seem merely to have come for the food – and not the sea at all!

by the sea

three-flavoured fish
pla sam rut

4 large garlic cloves, finely chopped

2 large fresh red chillies, finely chopped

1 medium-size, firm-fleshed fish suitable for deep-frying (bream or sea bass would do), cleaned

vegetable oil for deep-frying, plus 2 tablespoons extra for stir-frying

2 tablespoons palm sugar (see page 20)

3 tablespoons fish sauce

2 tablespoons tamarind water (see page 21)

1 In a mortar, pound the garlic and chillies together to form a paste. Set aside.

2 Rinse the fish and pat dry with kitchen paper.

3 Heat the oil in a deep-fryer to 200°C (400°F) and deep-fry the fish until golden brown and crispy. Drain on kitchen paper and place on a serving dish to keep hot.

4 Heat 2 tablespoons of oil in a wok or frying pan and stir in the pounded garlic and chilli paste. Add the palm sugar and stir, then stir in the fish sauce and tamarind water. Pour over the deep-fried fish and serve immediately.

hot and sour soup with prawns and lemon grass tom yam gung

The pungent flavour of lemon grass has made this the most popular Thai soup. Actually, we don't eat it as soup, but instead pour a little on our rice as a flavouring while eating our main meal. I've put it in this chapter because we like to eat it when we arrive at the coast as it clears the sinuses – all the better to enjoy the bracing sea air.

500ml (18fl oz) chicken stock

1 tablespoon grilled chilli oil (*tom yam* sauce – see page 26)

2 kaffir lime leaves, finely chopped

5cm (2in) piece of tender lemon grass, roughly chopped

3 tablespoons lemon juice

3 tablespoons fish sauce

1–2 small fresh red or green chillies, roughly chopped

1/2 teaspoon granulated sugar

8 straw mushrooms, halved (tinned mushrooms will do)

225g (8oz) raw prawns, peeled and de-veined

1 In a large saucepan, heat the stock with the tom yam sauce.

2 Add the lime leaves, lemon grass, lemon juice, fish sauce, chillies and sugar, then bring to the boil and simmer for 2 minutes. Stir in the mushrooms and prawns and cook for a further 2–3 minutes, or until the prawns are cooked through.

3 Pour into soup bowls and serve.

steamed mussels with lemon grass
hoy op

If you like French moules marinières, you'll probably find this dish shares some of its qualities – not least that it has a light, refreshing flavour and is just as easy to cook. Another thing it shares with its French counterpart is that it is rather good served with a cold beer.

for the dipping sauce

2 tablespoons lemon juice

2 tablespoons fish sauce

1 teaspoon granulated sugar

4 small fresh red or green chillies, finely chopped

1 tablespoon crushed roasted peanuts

for the mussels

450g (1lb) fresh mussels, soaked overnight in cold water with a
   handful of porridge oats to aid the self-cleaning process

60g (2oz) lemon grass, cut into fine matchsticks

20 fresh holy basil leaves

The author buying street food in Nakhon Pathom
before moving on to Hua Hin.

1 First make the sauce. Place all the ingredients in a small serving dish and mix well together. Set aside.

2 Next prepare the mussels. Rinse in clean cold water at least 3 times, then scrub thoroughly under cold running water, scraping off any barnacles or 'beards'. At every stage, discard any mussels that do not close when shaken or float to the surface of the water.

3 Place the mussels in a heavy-based pan on a high heat. Throw in the lemon grass and basil leaves and stir, then cover the pan with a lid. Shake the pan carefully from side to side to toss the mussels in the liquid that has collected at the bottom, and to spread the ingredients. Continue to cook for 5–8 minutes, or until the shells have opened, shaking the pan occasionally.

4 Ladle on to a serving dish, discarding any mussels that haven't opened. To eat, remove the mussels from their shells and dip in the sauce.

fried rice with pineapple
khao pad supparot

This is sometimes served in a scooped-out pineapple, either halved lengthways or hollowed-out whole with the top replaced. Its delicate sweetness makes it a particularly good accompaniment to seafood.

2 tablespoons vegetable oil

1 garlic clove, finely chopped

60g (2oz) dried black fungus mushrooms (see page 17), soaked in cold water for 10 minutes and cut into small pieces

60g (2oz) chopped onion

85g (3oz) pineapple chunks

225g (8oz) cooked fragrant rice

3 tablespoons light soy sauce

1/2 teaspoon granulated sugar

1/2 teaspoon ground white pepper

30g (1oz) roasted cashew nuts

to garnish

1 spring onion, finely chopped into rings

a few fresh coriander leaves

1 In a wok or frying pan, heat the oil until a light haze appears. Add the garlic and fry until golden brown. Stirring all the time, add the mushrooms, onion, pineapple, rice, soy sauce, sugar and pepper.

2 Add the cashew nuts, stir once and turn onto a serving dish. Garnish with a sprinkling of spring onion rings and fresh coriander leaves and serve.

puffed bread roti

350g (12oz) plain flour

2 tablespoons caster sugar

1 egg, lightly beaten

225ml (8fl oz) cold water

6 tablespoons vegetable oil (you may not need all of this)

1 To make the dough, combine the flour and sugar in a bowl. Make a well in the centre, break in the egg and pour in the water. Combine everything together with your fingers and knead to a smooth dough.

2 Divide the dough into 10 balls. Using a rolling pin, press out each ball to make a round pancake – this should be as thin as possible, while still holding together when lifted from the lightly floured board.

3 Heat a griddle or frying pan, add enough oil to grease the surface and, when this is sizzling hot, fry the pancakes until crisp and golden brown, turning once. The Roti will puff up as they cook, creating a mottled effect with dark brown patches. Serve on their own as a snack; as an Indian-style accompaniment to curry; or as a dessert, dipped in sugar or condensed milk.

chicken with curry powder
gai pad pong kari

2 tablespoons vegetable oil

2 garlic cloves, finely chopped

1 teaspoon curry powder

100g (4oz) chicken breast, de-boned and cut into small pieces

1 small onion, chopped

1 medium potato, cut into small dice

about 8 tablespoons chicken stock or water

2 tablespoons fish sauce

a pinch of sugar

4 tablespoons coconut milk

1 In a wok or frying pan, heat the oil and fry the garlic until golden brown.

2 Add the curry powder, stir to mix thoroughly and cook for 1 minute. Add the chicken and stir well to coat the meat in the curry mixture. Add the onion, potato and 4 tablespoons stock or water and stir-fry over a medium heat until the potato is just cooked. If the mixture becomes dry, add a little more stock or water.

3 Stir in the fish sauce, sugar and coconut milk and simmer gently until the sauce thickens.

4 Turn into a bowl and serve.

fried rice with prawns and chillies
khao pad prik gung

2 tablespoons vegetable oil

2 garlic cloves, finely chopped

2 small fresh red chillies, finely chopped

100g (4oz) peeled raw prawns

1 tablespoon fish sauce

$1/4$ teaspoon granulated sugar

1 tablespoon light soy sauce

450g (1lb) cooked fragrant rice

$1/2$ small onion, slivered

$1/2$ red or green sweet pepper, de-seeded and slivered

$1/2$ teaspoon ground white pepper

1 spring onion, green part only, slivered into 2.5cm (1in) lengths

to garnish
a few fresh coriander leaves

1 In a wok or frying pan, heat the oil and fry the garlic until golden brown.

2 Stir in the chillies and prawns, then add the fish sauce, sugar and soy sauce. Cook for a few seconds, stirring all the time, until the prawns are cooked through.

3 Add the cooked rice and stir well, then add the onion, sweet pepper, white pepper and spring onion. Stir quickly to mix, then turn on to a serving dish and garnish with the fresh coriander leaves.

deep-fried crab claws gam poo tod

for the plum sauce
1 whole preserved plum (see page 21)
225ml (8fl oz) rice or white wine vinegar
5 tablespoons granulated sugar

for the crab claws
85g (3oz) minced pork
100g (4oz) shelled and de-veined raw prawns, finely chopped
1 egg
1 garlic clove, finely chopped
1 tablespoon fish sauce
1 tablespoon oyster sauce
1 teaspoon cornflour
$1/2$ teaspoon ground white pepper
6–8 crab claws (depending on size)
vegetable oil for deep-frying

1 First make the plum sauce. With a fork, shred the flesh of the plum from its stone – this should leave you with tiny scrapings. Place the vinegar and sugar in a heavy-based saucepan and heat gently, stirring, to dissolve the sugar. Bring to the boil and boil rapidly to make a syrup. Stir in the plum scrapings, then pour into a serving dish and set aside.

2 To make the coating for the crab claws, thoroughly mix together the minced pork, chopped prawns, egg, garlic, fish sauce, oyster sauce, cornflour and white pepper. Divide the mixture by the number of crab claws (6–8) and mould a piece round the meaty section at the end of each claw, leaving the pincer shell exposed.

3 Heat the oil in a deep-fryer to 200°C (400°F) and fry the crab claws until the coating is deep golden brown. Remove, drain on kitchen paper and serve with the plum sauce.

massaman lamb curry
massaman gae

Although near the sea, we often eat as much meat as seafood in the South – probably because much of the population is Muslim and we're keen to try their Malaysian dishes with unusual spices. Best known is massaman or 'Muslim' curry, though it is now found all over Thailand.

250ml (9fl oz) coconut cream

2 tablespoons vegetable oil

1 garlic clove, finely chopped

1 tablespoon massaman curry paste (see page 26)

175g (6oz) lean lamb, cut into 2.5cm (1in) cubes

1 tablespoon tamarind water (see page 21) or 2 tablespoons lemon juice

1 teaspoon granulated sugar

3 tablespoons fish sauce

250ml (9fl oz) lamb or beef stock or water

2 small potatoes, quartered

2 tablespoons whole roasted peanuts

2 shallots, quartered

1 In a small pan, gently warm the coconut cream until it just starts to separate. Remove from the heat and set aside.

2 In a wok or frying pan, heat the oil and fry the garlic until golden brown. Add the curry paste, mix well and cook for a few seconds. Add half the warmed coconut cream and cook for 2–3 seconds, stirring all the time, until the mixture bubbles and starts to reduce.

3 Add the lamb and turn in the sauce to ensure that each piece is thoroughly coated. Stirring after each addition, add the tamarind water or lemon juice, sugar, fish sauce, stock or water and the remainder of the warmed coconut cream. Simmer gently for 15 minutes, stirring from time to time.

4 Add the quartered potatoes and simmer for a further 4 minutes. Add the peanuts and cook for 4 minutes more. Stir in the onions and cook for 2 more minutes, then pour into a serving dish and garnish with fresh coriander.

hot and sour seafood salad
yam talay

lettuce, fresh parsley and cucumber slices, or other firm leaves or raw vegetables in season, to make a salad

2 tablespoons lemon juice

2 small fresh red chillies, finely chopped

2 tablespoons fish stock

1 teaspoon granulated sugar

2 tablespoons fish sauce

4 fish balls (see page 19)

4 large raw prawns, shelled and de-veined

2–4 crab claws

4 pieces squid, cut into slices

2 kaffir lime leaves, finely sliced

1 shallot, finely chopped

1/2 small onion, finely slivered

a few sprigs of fresh coriander, coarsely chopped

1 Prepare a seasonal salad and place in a serving dish. Set aside.

2 In a wok or frying pan, mix together the lemon juice, chillies, stock, sugar and fish sauce. Bring to the boil, stirring all the time.

3 Add the fish balls, prawns, crab claws and squid and stir-fry for a minute or two, or until cooked through. Remove from the heat and stir in the lime leaves, shallot, onion and fresh coriander. Pour over the prepared salad and serve immediately.

squid with dry curry patpet plamuk

175–225g (6–8oz) squid (bodies only), washed and cleaned

2 tablespoons vegetable oil

2 garlic cloves, finely chopped

2 teaspoons red curry paste (see page 25)

1 tablespoon fish sauce

1 tablespoon light soy sauce

1 teaspoon granulated sugar

2–3 small green aubergines (see page 15), quartered

1 small fresh red chilli, finely chopped

2 kaffir lime leaves, finely sliced

10 fresh holy basil leaves

1 Score the squid quite finely on both sides, then cut into pieces about 2.5cm (1in) square. Set aside.

2 In a wok or frying pan, heat the oil and fry the garlic until golden brown. Stir in the curry paste and cook for a few seconds. Add the squid, coating it in the sauce. Add the fish sauce, soy sauce, sugar and aubergines and stir-fry over a high heat until the aubergines are cooked through. Now stir in the chilli, lime leaves and basil.

3 When the squid is cooked through and opaque, give the dish a final stir and pour into a serving dish.

sweetcorn cakes
thod man khao phod

This a vegetarian dish, normally served on the island of Phuket during the annual vegetarian festival – the largest in Thailand. Far from being a gentle herbivores reunion, the festival has some sort of strange religious basis that is marked by scenes of ritual self-punishment with participants walking through fire and sticking sharpened rods into themselves, all in a trance-like state. Definitely not for me.

for the cakes

1 tablespoon red curry paste (see page 25)

150g (5oz) sweetcorn kernels (tinned or frozen)

1 tablespoon light soy sauce

1 teaspoon granulated sugar

5–6 French beans, finely sliced

2 kaffir lime leaves, finely sliced

2 tablespoons dried breadcrumbs

vegetable oil for deep-frying

for the hot and sour peanut sauce

4 tablespoons rice or white wine vinegar

2 tablespoons granulated sugar

2.5cm (1in) piece of English cucumber, quartered lengthways and finely sliced

2 shallots, finely sliced

1 tablespoon crushed roasted peanuts

1–2 small fresh red chillies, finely sliced

1 Combine the ingredients for the sweetcorn cakes in a bowl and set aside.

2 To make the sauce, place the vinegar and sugar in a small saucepan and stir over a low heat until the sugar has dissolved. Bring to the boil and boil rapidly until the sauce begins to thicken slightly. Remove from the heat, pour into a small bowl and leave to cool completely.

3 Divide the sweetcorn mixture into 6 portions and form into small patties with your hands.

4 Heat the oil in a deep-fryer to 200°C (400°F). While the oil is heating, stir all the remaining sauce ingredients into the syrup and set aside.

5 Fry the patties in the hot oil until golden brown. Remove, drain on kitchen paper and serve with the sauce.

prawn spring rolls po pea gung

To me this is just one of many pleasant, simple, inexpensive nibbles you get on most beaches in Thailand – although I must admit its rather elegant appearance makes it look classier than the average snack. You can now find it on the menu at many fashionable restaurants – and at highly inflated prices.

for the marinade

2 large garlic cloves, finely chopped

1 tablespoon fish sauce

1 tablespoon light soy sauce

1 tablespoon oyster sauce

1/2 teaspoon ground white pepper

1 teaspoon granulated sugar

for the spring rolls

10 large raw king prawns, shelled (leaving tail shells on) and de-veined

10 spring roll sheets, about 7.5cm (3in) square

vegetable oil for deep-frying

a little egg wash, for sealing

for the sweet chilli sauce

4 tablespoons granulated sugar

6 tablespoons rice or white wine vinegar

$1/_2$ teaspoon salt

2 small fresh red chillies, finely chopped

1 Combine the ingredients for the marinade in a bowl, stir in the prawns, coating them well in the sauce, and leave to marinate while you complete the other tasks.

2 To make the chilli sauce, place the sugar and vinegar in a small saucepan and heat gently, stirring, until the sugar dissolves. Bring to the boil and boil rapidly until the sauce starts to thicken. Remove from the heat, stir in the salt and chopped chillies and pour into a small bowl. Set aside.

3 Lay the spring roll sheets on a work surface. Place a marinated prawn in the centre of each sheet and roll up tightly. Brush a little egg wash on the open edge to seal it. Discard the marinade.

4 Heat the oil in a deep-fryer to 200°C (400°F). Fry the spring rolls until pale golden brown, then remove and drain on kitchen paper. Serve with the sweet chilli sauce.

stir-fried seafood with garlic and peppercorns

talay pad kratiam prik thai

This is one of those dishes that turns the economics of cooking completely on its head and is reason enough to visit Thailand. In the West, seafood is expensive and fresh peppercorns prohibitively so, yet somewhere like the street food market along the road leading up to the old Railway Hotel in the seaside resort of Hua Hin, it costs only a few coins. As they say in the Michelin guides: 'worth the detour'.

2 tablespoons vegetable oil

3 garlic cloves, finely chopped

70g (2^1/$_2$oz) squid, cleaned and cut into 2cm (^{3}/$_4$in) pieces

4 raw king prawns, shelled and de-veined

4 scallops

4 crab claws, bashed

1 tablespoon fish sauce

1 tablespoon oyster sauce

1 tablespoon light soy sauce

^{1}/$_2$ teaspoon granulated sugar

^{1}/$_2$ teaspoon ground white pepper

60g (2oz) fresh green peppercorns, kept on their stalks and cooked in small bunches

1 In a wok or frying pan, heat the oil and fry the garlic until golden brown.

2 Add the seafood with the remaining ingredients and stir-fry over a high heat for 2–3 minutes. Transfer to a serving dish.

barbecued squid plamuk yang

Sold on nearly every beach around Thailand, the aroma of grilling squid instantly evokes sea, sand and holidays. At the seaside, I always have some at the end of the day with a beer or a whisky as an aperitif before my evening meal.

2 large squid (bodies about 15–23cm/6–9in long), cleaned, with the sac and tentacles separated

for the three-flavour sauce

2 tablespoons fish sauce

3 tablespoons lemon juice

2 large garlic cloves, finely chopped

2 small fresh green chillies, finely chopped

2 teaspoons granulated sugar

1 Preheat the barbecue or grill to medium.

2 Cut each squid body sac lengthways into quarters and rinse under a tap. With a sharp knife, lightly score each side of the squid body diagonally into a diamond pattern (this will help the cooking process and make the final dish more attractive). Leave the tentacles whole for grilling or barbecuing – although they can be cut up after cooking.

3 Lay all the squid pieces under the grill or on the barbecue and cook for 10 minutes on each side, or until well-browned; the body pieces should curl up.

4 While the squid is cooking, make the sauce. Combine the fish sauce, lemon juice, chopped garlic, chillies and sugar in a small bowl and set aside.

5 To serve, arrange the cooked squid on a large dish and place the bowl of sauce in the middle. Dip the squid pieces into the sauce and eat with your fingers.

prawns in batter with two sauces
gung tod

You may not intend to eat on the beach, but when these turn up, carried on a tray by a strolling vendor, it's surprising how they whet the appetite. The batter and sauces are also suitable for making deep-fried tempura vegetables – carrots, celery, beans and courgettes all work well.

for the chilli-vinegar sauce
4 tablespoons rice or white wine vinegar
4 tablespoons granulated sugar
1/4 teaspoon salt
1 small fresh red or green chilli, finely chopped

for the coriander-soy sauce
3 tablespoons light soy sauce
5–6 fresh coriander leaves, coarsely chopped

for the prawns in batter
150g (5oz) plain flour
1/2 teaspoon salt
1 egg
225ml (8fl oz) water
vegetable oil for deep-frying
12 large raw prawns, de-headed, shelled and de-veined (keep tail shell on)

1 First make the chilli-vinegar sauce. Place the vinegar and sugar in a small saucepan and heat gently, stirring, until the sugar dissolves. Bring to the boil and boil rapidly to form a syrup. Stir in the salt, remove from the heat and pour into a serving dish to cool. Add the chopped chilli. Set aside.

2 To make the coriander-soy sauce, combine the soy sauce with the coriander leaves and pour into a small bowl. Set aside.

3 For the batter, combine the flour and salt in a bowl. Make a well in the centre and break in the egg. Add the water gradually, whisking constantly, to give a thick, creamy batter.

4 Heat the oil in a deep-fryer to 200°C (400°F) or until a light haze appears. Dip each prawn into the batter, making sure it is thoroughly coated, and drop into the hot oil. Deep-fry until golden brown. Remove with a strainer or slotted spoon and drain on kitchen paper. Arrange on a serving dish.

5 To eat, hold the prawns by the tail and dip into either sauce.

beancurd sheet stuffed with crab
hoi joh

for the crab parcels
4–5 beancurd sheets (about 15 x 30cm/6 x 12in), see page 19
175g (6oz) crabmeat
60g (2oz) minced pork
2 garlic cloves, finely chopped
1 egg
1 tablespoon light soy sauce
$1/2$ teaspoon ground white pepper
1 teaspoon granulated sugar
a pinch of salt
vegetable oil for deep-frying

for the plum sauce
1 small preserved plum (see page 21)
6 tablespoons rice or white wine vinegar
4 tablespoons granulated sugar

to garnish
lettuce leaves and finely sliced cucumber

1 First make the crab parcels. Soak the beancurd sheets in cold water for 5–6 minutes, or until soft and pliable. (Handle with care as they are prone to tearing.) Set aside.

2 To make the filling, combine the crabmeat, pork, garlic, egg, soy sauce, pepper, sugar and salt in a bowl.

3 Place the soaked beancurd sheets on a work surface and divide the filling between each. Roll the sheets up to form sausage shapes, folding in the ends. You should end up with 4–5 wrapped sausages about 12cm ($4^{1}/_{2}$in) in length. Tie the sausage parcels at intervals with cotton thread to divide into 4–5 sections. Place in a preheated steamer and steam for 10 minutes, during which time the beancurd will tighten around the filling.

4 Remove from the steamer and allow to cool. If you are preparing the Hoi Joh in advance, you can now place the parcels in the refrigerator for cooking later that day, or even the following day. They may also be frozen at this stage.

5 To make the plum sauce, place all the ingredients in a small saucepan and heat gently, stirring, until the sugar has dissolved. Bring to the boil and boil rapidly to form a thin syrup. Check for flavour – the sauce should be sweet and sour – and pour into a serving dish.

6 To finish, cut the beancurd parcels where they are tied with cotton and remove the thread. You will now have 16–20 roughly ball-shaped pieces. Heat the oil in a deep-fryer to 200°C (400°F) and fry the pieces until golden brown. Arrange the deep-fried balls on a serving plate lined with lettuce and finely sliced cucumber and serve with the plum sauce.

clams with chilli and basil
hoy lai pad nam prik pow

450g (1lb) fresh baby clams in their shells

2 tablespoons vegetable oil

2 garlic cloves, finely chopped

1 tablespoon grilled chilli oil (*nam prik pao*, see page 26)

2 tablespoons fish sauce

2 tablespoons fish stock or water

1/2 teaspoon granulated sugar

1 long fresh red chilli, finely slivered

20 fresh holy basil leaves, shredded

1 Rinse the clams under cold water, discarding any that do not close when shaken. Drain and set aside.

2 In a wok or frying pan, heat the oil and fry the garlic until golden brown. Add the clams and chilli oil and stir thoroughly. Add all the remaining ingredients in turn, stirring after each addition, and cook over a high heat until the clams open. Discard any clams that remain closed.

3 Pour into a serving bowl and serve.

stir-fried seafood with roast chilli paste talay pad prik pao

2 tablespoons vegetable oil

3 garlic cloves, finely chopped

1 tablespoon grilled chilli oil (*nam prik pao*, see page 26)

4 raw king prawns, shelled and de-veined

4 scallops

4 mussels

4 crab claws

30g (1oz) squid, cut into 2cm (3/4in) pieces

1 stick celery, sliced

1 carrot about 4cm (1¹/2in) long, cut into slices

30g (1oz) mixed red, yellow and green sweet peppers, de-seeded and sliced

1 tablespoon oyster sauce

1 tablespoon fish sauce

1 teaspoon granulated sugar

1 In a wok or frying pan, heat the oil and fry the garlic until golden brown.

2 Add the chilli oil and stir well, then toss in the seafood and stir-fry for about 2 minutes.

3 Add the vegetables with the remaining ingredients and stir-fry for 1 minute. Transfer to a serving dish and serve.

sweet and sour beancurd tao hou peaw wan

This is a classic vegetarian dish served on its own, but its light, varied flavours also make it good to serve with seafood dishes, particularly hot ones like Stir-Fried Seafood with Roast Chilli Paste (see recipe opposite).

vegetable oil for deep-frying, plus 2 tablespoons for stir-frying

100g (4oz) beancurd (see page 19), cut into 5cm (2in) cubes

2 garlic cloves, finely chopped

30g (1oz) English cucumber, sliced

30g (1oz) mixed red, yellow and green sweet peppers, sliced

3–4 button mushrooms, quartered

4–5 baby sweetcorn, quartered lengthways

2 spring onions, cut into 2cm (3/4in) lengths

1 medium tomato, sliced into rounds

30g (1oz) pineapple chunks

2 tablespoons granulated sugar

2 tablespoons white wine vinegar

1 teaspoon salt

1 Heat the oil in a deep-fryer to 200°C (400°F). Deep-fry the beancurd cubes until golden brown, then remove and drain on kitchen paper.

2 In a wok or frying pan, heat the oil and fry the garlic until golden brown. Add all the vegetables and the pineapple, stir well, then add the sugar, vinegar and salt. Stir-fry over a high heat for 30 seconds.

3 Toss in the deep-fried beancurd, stir once, then turn onto a serving dish.

Bangkokians love to go to Chaing Mai because the climate is cooler, but there is also the food which is much appreciated and sought out. Here we can see a parade of boys dressed in historical military costumes, resting by a stall selling sweets during the Inthakin Festival at Wat Chedi Luang.

chiang mai spicy dip
nam prik num

The Thai language is full of double meanings. In this dish, for example, '*Num*' can mean a young man and the recipe calls for young chillies which are thought to be particularly lusty.

2 large fresh green chillies

4 small fresh green chillies

4 large garlic cloves, peeled

4 small shallots, peeled

2 medium tomatoes

5 round green aubergines (see page 15)

2 tablespoons lemon juice

2 tablespoons fish sauce

1/2 teaspoon salt

1 teaspoon granulated sugar

1 Preheat the grill to medium.

2 Wrap the chillies, garlic, shallots, tomatoes and aubergines in foil and place under the grill. Cook until they begin to soften, turning once or twice. Unwrap, place in a mortar and pound together to form a liquid paste.

3 Add the lemon juice, fish sauce, salt and sugar to the paste, stirring well.

4 Turn into a small bowl. Serve as a dip, surrounded by crisp salad ingredients – crisp lettuce, cucumber, radish and celery – or with raw or blanched vegetables.

curried pork with pickled garlic
gaeng haeng lay

This shows the influence of neighbouring Burma and, through Burma, of India on Thai cuisine. There are many Burmese cultural influences in the northwest, particularly on religious ceremonies but also on craftwork such as woodcarving, at which the Burmese excel. Indeed, many of the things on sale in northern Thai craft shops may have been made in Burma and smuggled across the border.

2 tablespoons vegetable oil

1 garlic clove, finely chopped

1 tablespoon red curry paste (see page 25)

125ml (4fl oz) coconut cream

100g (4oz) boneless pork with a little fat, finely slivered

2.5cm (1in) piece of fresh ginger, peeled and finely chopped

2 tablespoons chicken stock or water

2 tablespoons fish sauce

1 teaspoon granulated sugar

1/2 teaspoon turmeric powder

2 teaspoons lemon juice

4 pickled garlic cloves (see page 20), finely chopped

1 In a wok or frying pan, heat the oil and fry the garlic until golden brown. Add the curry paste and stir well. Pour in the coconut cream and stir until the liquid begins to reduce and thicken. Do not boil.

2 Add the pork and stir-fry over a high heat until cooked through – approximately 1 minute. Add all the remaining ingredients in turn, stirring constantly.

3 Turn into a serving bowl and serve.

chicken curry noodle with pickled cabbage kow soi

Originally from Burma, this has become the single most popular dish in and around the northern Thai capital Chiang Mai. This is where each of my friends seems to have his or her favourite street seller, who they insist I visit. They get quite passionate in defence of their vendor and we often end up arguing by the road as to where we should eat – much the most enjoyable sort of argument to have.

100g (4oz) fresh *ba mee* noodles (see page 24), or use 60g (2oz) dry noodles, soaked and drained

2 tablespoons vegetable oil

1 small garlic clove, finely chopped

1 teaspoon red curry paste (see page 25)

125ml (4fl oz) coconut cream

175g (6oz) boneless chicken breast or thigh, cut into thin strips

225ml (8fl oz) chicken stock

1 teaspoon curry powder

2 tablespoons fish sauce

1/2 teaspoon lemon juice

1/2 teaspoon granulated sugar

to garnish

1 spring onion, coarsely chopped

2 shallots, finely diced

1 tablespoon pickled cabbage (*pak gat dong*, see page 20), thinly sliced

1 lemon, cut into wedges

1 Bring a saucepan of water to the boil. Using a sieve or mesh strainer, dip the noodles into the water for 2–3 seconds, just to heat them through. Drain and set aside in a serving bowl.

2 In a wok or frying pan, heat the oil and fry the garlic until golden brown. Stir in the curry paste and cook for a few seconds. Pour in the coconut cream and cook until the liquid starts to reduce and thicken. Do not boil. Add the chicken and stir-fry for a minute or two, then add the chicken stock, curry powder, fish sauce, lemon juice and sugar, stirring constantly.

3 Pour the chicken mixture over the noodles, garnish with spring onion, shallots and pickled cabbage and serve with the lemon wedges on the side.

A line of food stalls, lit up for the night, in front of Wat Pan Tow.

deep-fried spare ribs grat dook moo tod

This is good with sticky rice and perfect when travelling, as it can be eaten cold with your fingers. Look out for it at transport stops.

4 garlic cloves, roughly chopped

4 large coriander roots, roughly chopped

2 tablespoons plain flour

1 egg

2 tablespoons fish sauce

2 tablespoons light soy sauce

450g (1lb) pork spare ribs, chopped into 4–5cm (1¹/₂–2in) pieces

vegetable oil for deep-frying

1 Using a pestle and mortar or a blender, pound or blend the garlic and coriander roots together and set aside.

2 In a large bowl, mix together the flour with the egg, fish sauce and soy sauce. Add the garlic and coriander paste and mix thoroughly. Add the spare rib pieces and coat well with the mixture. Leave to marinate for at least 30 minutes.

3 Heat the oil in a deep-fryer to 200°C (400°F) or until a light haze appears. Deep-fry the pieces of rib for 6–8 minutes, or until dark golden brown. Remove with a slotted spoon, drain on kitchen paper and serve.

fried fish with turmeric
pla tod khamin

This is usually made with freshwater fish. In the north, vendors lay the fish out in a line for you to choose from and give you the sauce in a little plastic bag, so that you can put it over the fish when you want. Surprisingly, though cold, the fish is still crispy. It's another useful dish for travellers with limited equipment, though you will need a spoon.

1 medium-size, firm-fleshed fish (bream or sea bass would do) or 2 fillets
5cm (2in) piece of fresh turmeric (see page 18), peeled, roughly chopped
1 tablespoon black peppercorns
2 large garlic cloves, roughly chopped
1 tablespoon roughly chopped shallots
1 tablespoon fish sauce
1 tablespoon granulated sugar
3 tablespoons vegetable oil

to garnish
a few fresh coriander leaves

1 Clean the fish and cut into 5cm (2in) pieces.

2 In a mortar, pound together the turmeric, peppercorns, garlic and shallots to form a paste.

3 Place the pieces of fish in a bowl with the paste, fish sauce and sugar. Mix well, spreading the mixture all over the fish.

4 Heat the oil in a frying pan and fry the fish until crisp and golden brown.

5 Drain on kitchen paper and arrange on a serving dish. Garnish with fresh coriander and serve.

fried rice with pork
khao pad moo

1 tablespoon vegetable oil
2 garlic cloves, finely chopped
100g (4oz) lean pork, finely slivered
1 egg
225g (8oz) cooked fragrant rice
60g (2oz) broccoli, cut into small florets
1 tablespoon light soy sauce
a pinch of sugar
1 tablespoon fish sauce
ground white pepper, to season

1 Heat the oil in a wok or frying pan, add the garlic and fry until golden brown.

2 Add the pork and stir-fry briefly over a high heat. Break the egg into the pan and stir well. Add the rice, combine well, then stir in the broccoli.

3 Stirring constantly, add the soy sauce, sugar and fish sauce. Turn on to a serving dish, season with ground white pepper and serve.

fried curried rice
khao pad pong karl

2 tablespoons vegetable oil

1 garlic clove, finely chopped

225g (8oz) boiled rice

60g (2oz) potato, cut into 1cm (1/2in) dice

60g (2oz) onion, cut into small dice

60g (2oz) peas

3 tablespoons light soy sauce

1/2 teaspoon granulated sugar

1 teaspoon curry powder

1/2 teaspoon ground white pepper

to garnish

2.5cm (1in) piece of English cucumber, finely sliced into rounds

a few fresh coriander leaves

1 In a wok or frying pan, heat the oil until a light haze appears, add the garlic and fry until golden brown. Add the boiled rice, stir once, then add all the remaining ingredients and stir-fry until the potato is cooked through.

2 Turn on to a serving dish and garnish with cucumber slices and fresh coriander.

Woman preparing fish ball soup at the Long Yan Market (*Talat Lam Yai*), Chiang Mai.

egg noodles with stir-fried vegetables mee sua

100g (4oz) *ba mee* noodles (see page 24), dried or fresh

2 tablespoons vegetable oil

1 garlic clove, finely chopped

1 large dried red chilli, roughly chopped

60g (2oz) celery, finely chopped

60g (2oz) beansprouts

2 spring onions, finely chopped

1 medium tomato, cut into segments

1/2 teaspoon chilli powder

3 tablespoons light soy sauce

1 teaspoon dark soy sauce

1/2 teaspoon granulated sugar

1 Bring a pan of water to the boil for the noodles. If using fresh noodles, shake the strands loose, place in a sieve or strainer and lower into the boiling water for 2–3 seconds, or until heated through. If using dried noodles, cook in the boiling water until the strands separate, by which time they will be soft. Drain and set aside.

2 In a wok, heat the oil until a light haze appears. Add the garlic and fry for 2–3 seconds, then add the chilli and continue to stir-fry until the garlic is golden brown.

3 Add the cooked noodles to the pan, stir well to prevent them from sticking, then add all the remaining ingredients, stirring quickly. Turn on to a serving dish and serve.

white radish cake with beansprouts kanom pad ga

(serves 3–4 – see page 14)

This recipe is prepared in two distinct stages: first the cake is made, then it is re-cooked with beansprouts, as here, or with other ingredients. This dish goes well with *Prik Nam Som* (see pages 24) or Sriracha Chilli Sauce.

for the cake
1 white radish (mooli, see page 18), weighing about 1kg (2lb)
175g (6oz) rice flour
2 tablespoons plain (wheat) flour
2 tablespoons water

1 Trim and peel the radish and cut into small cubes. Using a food processor or blender, mash the radish as finely as possible. This will have to be done in 2–3 batches. Place the mashed radish in a bowl and mix thoroughly with the rice and wheat flours and water.

2 Turn the mixture into a shallow tin or heatproof dish, about 20cm (8in) square: it should come about 2.5cm (1in) up the sides. Heat up your steamer (or use your largest saucepan with an upturned bowl in the bottom on which to rest the tin) and steam the cake for about 30 minutes from the time the steamer is hot. If you are using a thicker dish you will have to steam the cake for a little longer. When an inserted knife comes out clean, remove from the heat and allow to cool and dry out completely. The cake will set more solidly as it cools.

3 To serve, cut the cake into rectangles about 5 x 2.5cm (2 x 1in) size.

to finish the dish
3 tablespoons vegetable oil
1/2 batch white radish cake, cut into rectangles (see opposite)
2 garlic cloves, finely chopped
1 egg
2 tablespoons light soy sauce
1 tablespoon dark soy sauce
1/2 teaspoon granulated sugar
ground white pepper, to taste
30g (1oz) fresh beansprouts, rinsed and drained
3 spring onions, cut into 2.5cm (1in) slivers

1 In a frying pan (preferably non-stick), heat half the oil. Add the radish cake pieces and, stirring and turning constantly, fry until they are browned on all sides. Remove from the pan and set aside.

2 Add the rest of the oil to the pan and fry the garlic until golden brown. Break in the egg and cook for a few seconds, stirring all the time until the egg starts to set. Add the fried radish cake and mix well. Stir in both soy sauces, the sugar, pepper, beansprouts and spring onions, then turn onto a serving dish.

note
The remaining radish cake can be fried with other ingredients.

pork fried with chilli and nuts
moo pad prik haeng

2 tablespoons vegetable oil

1 garlic clove, finely chopped

5–6 long dried red chillies, with or without seeds, chopped

100g (4oz) lean pork, finely sliced

1 tablespoon fish sauce

1 heaped tablespoon whole roasted peanuts

6–8 small thin French beans, cut into 2.5cm (1in) lengths

3 tablespoons beef or vegetable stock

1 tablespoon light soy sauce

1/4 teaspoon granulated sugar

1 In a wok or frying pan, heat the oil and fry the garlic until golden brown. Add the chillies and stir. Add the pork and stir-fry over a high heat until the meat is slightly opaque.

2 Add all the remaining ingredients, one by one, stirring after each addition. Cook for another minute or two, making sure the meat is cooked through, then turn on to a serving dish.

minced beef noodle with curry
powder gueyteow nua sap

3 tablespoons vegetable oil

225g (8oz) (wet weight) soaked *sen lek* noodles (see page 24), rinsed and separated

1 teaspoon dark soy sauce

1 garlic clove, finely chopped

100g (4oz) lean minced beef

1 tablespoon chopped preserved radish (*chi po*, see page 21)

3 tablespoons beef stock, plus extra if necessary

1/2 teaspoon curry powder

1 small onion, finely slivered

1 tablespoon fish sauce

1 teaspoon cornflour mixed to a thin paste with water (you may not need all of this)

1 small spring onion, finely chopped

1 sprig of fresh coriander, coarsely chopped

to serve

crisp lettuce leaves

1 Line a serving dish with roughly torn lettuce leaves. Set aside.

2 Heat 2 tablespoons vegetable oil in a wok or frying pan. Add the noodles, stir quickly to prevent them from sticking, then add the dark soy sauce. Stir-fry for 30–60 seconds, then turn onto the prepared serving dish and set aside.

3 Add 1 more tablespoon of oil to the pan, add the garlic and fry until golden brown. Add the minced beef and stir-fry over a high heat until the

Men selling trays of fried insects, with the tower of Wat Mahawan in the background.

prawns with ginger
gung pad king

Even in the extreme North, seafood is very popular.

2 tablespoons vegetable oil

2 garlic cloves, finely chopped

2.5cm (1in) piece of fresh ginger, finely sliced

6–8 large raw prawns, peeled and de-veined

¼ teaspoon ground white pepper

1 tablespoon light soy sauce

1 tablespoon fish sauce

½ teaspoon granulated sugar

2 tablespoons chicken stock or water

2 spring onions, cut into 5cm (2in) lengths

1 small onion, sliced

1 In a wok or frying pan, heat the oil and fry the garlic until golden brown.

2 Stir in the ginger, then toss in the prawns. Stirring after each addition, add the pepper, soy sauce, fish sauce, sugar and stock or water. Stir-fry together for about 2 minutes, then add the spring onions and onion. Stir once, remove from the heat and turn on to a serving dish.

beef loses its red colour. Add the preserved radish, stock, curry powder, onion and fish sauce, stirring well after each addition. Thicken with a little of the cornflour and water paste, adding a little more stock if the mixture becomes too dry. Stir in the spring onion and fresh coriander and pour over the noodles.

for the curry

2 tablespoons vegetable oil

2 garlic cloves, finely chopped

1 tablespoon red curry paste (see page 25)

250ml (9fl oz) coconut milk

1 tablespoon fish sauce

2 teaspoons granulated sugar

30g (1oz) pineapple chunks, halved

3 cherry tomatoes, halved

6 seedless, green grapes (or pineapple chunks)

20 fresh sweet basil leaves

1 large fresh red chilli, sliced

1 Combine all the ingredients for the marinade in a bowl, add the duck, coating it well in the mixture and leave to marinate for 1 hour.

2 Preheat the grill to a high heat and grill the duck for 5 minutes on each side, or until it is seared on the outside but still pink on the inside. Leave to cool, then slice diagonally into thin pieces and set aside.

3 Make the curry. In a wok or frying pan, heat the oil and fry the garlic until golden brown. Stir in the curry paste, then add the coconut milk a little at a time – keep stirring – and bring to the boil.

4 Turn the heat down to a gentle simmer and stir in the fish sauce and sugar. Simmer for 5 minutes, then add the slices of duck.

5 Stir in the pineapple, tomatoes and grapes and simmer gently for 1 minute. Toss in the basil leaves and chilli, stir briefly, then transfer to a serving dish.

roast duck curry
gaeng phed ped yang

for the marinade

1 garlic clove, finely chopped

1 teaspoon finely chopped coriander root

1/2 teaspoon ground cumin

1 tablespoon fish sauce

1/2 teaspoon granulated sugar

175g (6oz) duck breast, de-boned

hot and sour vermicelli salad

yam wun sen

1 tablespoon vegetable oil

1 garlic clove, finely chopped

4 tablespoons chicken stock, plus extra if necessary

2 tablespoons lemon juice

2 tablespoons fish sauce

60g (2oz) lean minced pork

4 large raw prawns, shelled and de-veined

1/2 teaspoon chilli powder

1 teaspoon granulated sugar

6–8 pieces dried mushroom, soaked in water for 20 minutes

100g (4oz) dry *wun sen* noodles (see page 24), soaked in water for 20
   minutes, then drained

2 shallots, finely sliced

1 spring onion, chopped

to serve
lettuce and fresh parsley

to garnish
fresh coriander, coarsely chopped

1 Line a serving dish with lettuce and parsley and set aside.

2 In a small frying pan, heat the oil and fry the garlic until golden brown. Set aside, reserving the oil with the garlic.

3 In a saucepan, heat the stock, lemon juice and fish sauce and bring to the boil. Add the minced pork, stirring continuously until cooked through. Add the prawns and stir, then add the chilli powder and sugar. Simmer gently for 15–20 seconds, or until the prawns are opaque and cooked through. Add a little more stock or water if necessary to make up to 6–8 tablespoons.

4 Stir in the soaked mushroom pieces, noodles, shallots and spring onion and cook for a few more seconds, stirring constantly, or until the noodles are cooked through and hot. Turn on to the prepared dish and drizzle over the reserved garlic oil. Garnish with fresh coriander.

Night stall selling *roti* in front of Wat Mahawan.

baby clams with black bean sauce
hoy pat tow jeow

2 tablespoons vegetable oil

2 garlic cloves, finely chopped

450g (1lb) baby clams in their shells, scrubbed clean

2 tablespoons light soy sauce

1 small fresh red chilli, finely chopped

1 teaspoon black bean sauce

4 tablespoons water

10 fresh holy basil leaves

1 In a wok or frying pan, heat the oil, add the garlic and fry until golden brown.

2 Add the baby clams in their shells and stir thoroughly. Add the soy sauce, chilli, black bean sauce and water. Stir thoroughly, then add the basil. Cover with a lid and leave the clams to steam for a few minutes, shaking the pan occasionally from side to side, until the shells have opened.

3 Discard any clams that have not opened. Give the clams a final stir, to ensure that each one is covered by a little sauce and some chilli. Pull off the empty shell tops and discard, then arrange the open clams on a serving dish. Spoon over any remaining sauce and serve.

sausage fried with egg
nam pad kai

In Chiang Mai this would be made with Ba Yon, raw pork and garlic sausage. Ba Yon (Auntie Yon) was another street vendor whose product became so famous she ended up with her own factory. The northern garlic is so hot you'd think it was chilli and the uniquely round cloves 'cook' the raw pork à la Tahitienne. Don't worry – I've simplified this by specifying good old garlic sausage – not as spicy, but tasty nevertheless and certainly less of a health risk!

2 tablespoons vegetable oil

100g (4oz) garlic sausage, cut into 1cm (1/2in) slices

2 eggs

2 tablespoons fish sauce

1 whole head fresh garlic or 1 whole head pickled garlic (see page 20), peeled and finely sliced

1 large tomato, cut into wedges

3 spring onions, coarsely chopped

1 Heat the oil in a wok or frying pan, add the slices of sausage and stir-fry for a few seconds.

2 Break the eggs into the pan, mix briefly, then add the fish sauce, sliced garlic, tomato and spring onions. Stir-fry over a high heat for 2–3 seconds, then turn on to a serving dish.

pork in chilli sauce
nam prik ong

This Chiang Mai dip is sold on the street with bags of deep-fried pork rind – indeed, so much do they go together that there's a popular song about lovers having to be as close as pork and *Nam Prik Ong*.

2 tablespoons vegetable oil

2 garlic cloves, finely chopped

2 teaspoons red curry paste (see page 25)

100g (4oz) minced pork

1 large tomato, finely chopped

2 tablespoons fish sauce

1 tablespoon lemon juice

1 teaspoon granulated sugar

1 Heat the oil in a wok or frying pan, add the garlic and fry until golden brown.

2 Mix in the red curry paste and cook together briefly. Add the minced pork and stir-fry over a high heat until the meat loses its pink colour.

3 Add the tomato and stir-fry for 2–3 seconds, then add the fish sauce, lemon juice and sugar. Stir together for 2 minutes, then pour into a small bowl. Serve as a dip with raw vegetables.

steamed fish with chilli paste
oo pla

In northern Thailand, the street cook would normally wrap this in a banana leaf for steaming – but as the leaves only add flavour when they're grilled, I'm happy to steam this in an ordinary dish.

2 long dried red chillies, de-seeded and soaked in water to soften

3 garlic cloves, chopped

3 small red shallots, chopped

2.5cm (1in) piece of galangal (see page 17), peeled and coarsely chopped

1 tablespoon chopped lemon grass

450g (1lb) monk fish (or another freshwater fish), filleted and cut into 2.5cm (1in) chunks

2 tablespoons fish sauce

2 fresh sweet basil leaves

1 Using a pestle and mortar, pound together the chillies, garlic, shallots, galangal and lemon grass to make a paste.

2 Place the fish pieces in a mixing bowl with the fish sauce, basil leaves and paste and mix gently together.

3 Place the mixture in a heatproof bowl and steam for 15 minutes. Serve in the bowl.

2 If using small bananas, cut in half; if using large bananas, cut into 3 pieces. (You should end up with pieces about 7.5cm (3in) long.) Cut each piece in half lengthways to give strips about 1cm (¹/₂in) thick.

3 Heat the oil in a deep-fryer to 200°C (400°F). Dip the banana strips in the batter, shake off any excess and lower into the hot oil. Fry until golden brown, then remove, drain on kitchen paper and serve immediately.

sago and sweetcorn pudding
saku khao pohd

(serves 6–8, see page 14)

600ml (1 pint) water
2 teaspoons rosewater
100g (4oz) sago or tapioca
¹/₄ teaspoon salt
100g (4oz) granulated sugar
175g (6oz) sweetcorn kernels, tinned or frozen
100g (4oz) lotus seeds (see page 20)
125ml (4fl oz) coconut cream

1 In a medium saucepan, bring the water to the boil. Stir in the rosewater, sago or tapioca and salt and cook until the grains have fully swelled and are cooked through – about 15 minutes.

2 Add the sugar and simmer gently, stirring all the time, until the sugar has dissolved. Stir in the sweetcorn kernels and lotus seeds.

3 Divide the pudding between 6–8 small bowls, top each one with a spoonful of coconut cream, and serve warm.

banana fritters
kruay kaek

A personal favourite, now found all over southeast Asia. I last saw it being made in Lampang market, a banana growing centre near Chiang Mai, where a street cook was deep-frying masses of them in a gigantic wok. For 5 baht (about 30 pence) I got an enormous amount, wrapped in a sheet of old newspaper.

100g (4oz) plain flour
225ml (8fl oz) coconut milk
¹/₂ teaspoon salt
60g (2oz) granulated sugar
1 tablespoon white sesame seeds
6 small or 3 large unripe bananas (the skins just turning yellow)
vegetable oil for deep-frying

1 Combine the flour, coconut milk, salt, sugar and sesame seeds in a bowl and mix to form a smooth batter. Set aside.

the northeast

Issan, the north-eastern province of Thailand, was once considered a punishment post for Thai civil servants. People didn't visit it willingly; consequently the region has remained an unspoilt secret for many years. Recently, however, travelling food sellers have introduced a special new food from the north east to the streets of Bangkok – most notably grilled chicken and charcuterie. People have also discovered that the region has many unique religious festivals such as the monk-making ceremony at Ban Ta Klang, in which a procession of brightly caparisoned elephants traces its way from the river to the temple – helping themselves to titbits from the food stalls as they wander past!

spicy beef with dry-fried rice
nua namtok

225g (8oz) fillet steak, about 2.5cm (1in) thick

4 tablespoons beef stock

2 tablespoons fish sauce

4 tablespoons lemon juice

1 teaspoon granulated sugar

1 teaspoon chilli powder

2 spring onions, finely chopped

2 shallots, finely chopped

1 tablespoon dry-fried rice (see page 29), coarsely pounded

to garnish

a few fresh coriander leaves

1 Preheat a moderate-to-hot grill and grill the steak for 1–2 minutes on each side, depending on personal preference. Transfer to a chopping board and slice thinly, retaining any juices.

2 Place the sliced beef and any juices in a saucepan with the stock and heat gently. Stir in the fish sauce, lemon juice, sugar and chilli powder.

3 Remove from the heat, stir in the spring onions, shallots and pounded dry-fried rice and transfer to a serving bowl. Garnish with fresh coriander and serve.

beef stewed with noodle
gueyteow nua peui

1 litre (1¾ pints) beef stock

450g (1lb) lean rump steak, cut into 1cm (½in) cubes

3 garlic cloves, roughly chopped

3 coriander roots

2 cinnamon sticks

4 star anise

2 tablespoons light soy sauce

2 tablespoons fish sauce

1 teaspoon granulated sugar

85g (3oz) *sen mee* noodles (see page 24), soaked and drained

100g (4oz) fresh beansprouts

to garnish

1 spring onion, finely chopped

a few fresh coriander leaves, roughly chopped

1 Pour the stock into a large saucepan. Add the beef, garlic, coriander roots, cinnamon, star anise, soy sauce, fish sauce and sugar. Bring to the boil and simmer gently for 30 minutes. Skim off the scum occasionally.

2 In the meantime, put the noodles and beansprouts into a serving bowl. When the beef is cooked, pour the soup over the noodles and beansprouts, which will then cook in the hot stock.

3 Garnish with the chopped spring onion and fresh coriander and serve.

Sen mee or rice vermicelli noodles.

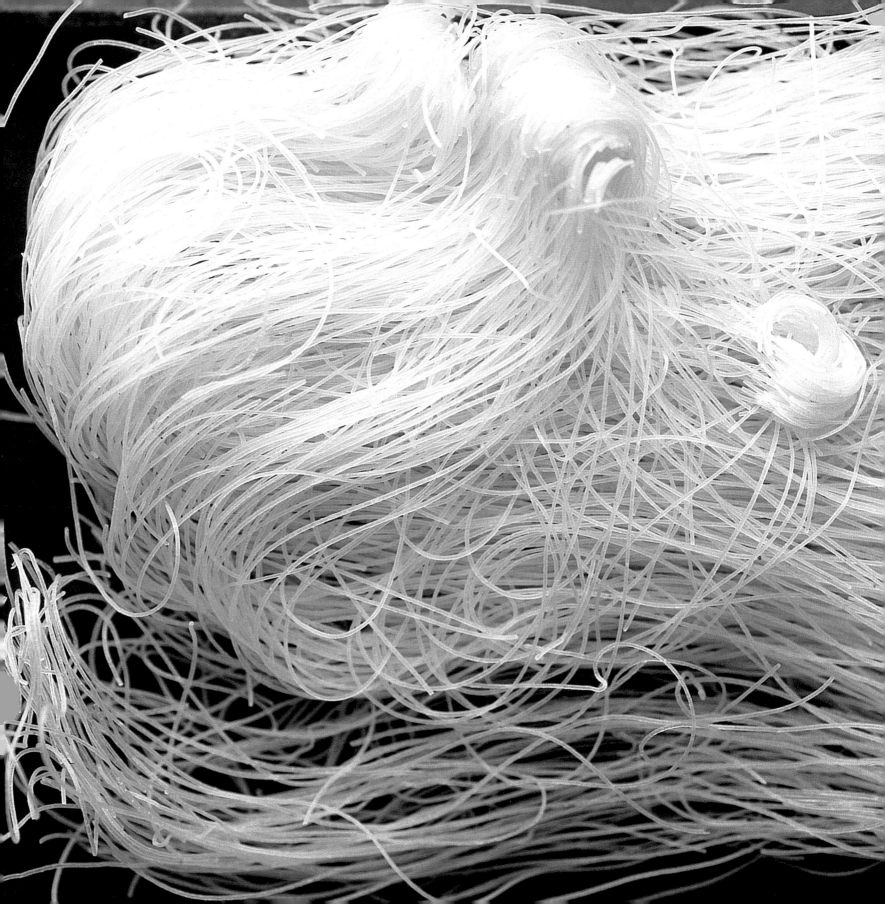

isan sausage si grot issan

Although many types of charcuterie are made in Isan, you see street stalls grilling these sausages everywhere. You buy one on a stick and eat it as you walk along, and if you can balance it, you have a little package of chopped chilli, nuts, ginger and coriander leaves – a real treat. They are popular among foreign visitors who like the fact that the sausage is freshly grilled and largely untouched by hand.

2 teaspoons finely chopped coriander root
225g (8oz) pork belly with fat, minced
450g (1lb) boiled fragrant rice
100g (4oz) garlic, finely chopped
1 teaspoon salt
about 75cm (29½in) sausage skin

1 Place the ingredients for the sausage filling in a bowl and mix together.

2 Put a funnel into 1 end of the tube of sausage skin and tie a knot in the other end. Force enough sausage meat into the skin to form a 7.5cm (3in) length and knead it down to the knotted end. When it is firmly packed, tie a knot in the tube close to the filling. Repeat this process until all the sausage meat is used up – you should end up with a string of 5 or 6 sausages. Prick any air bubbles to release the air.

3 Hang the string to dry in a well-ventilated, dry room – you can cook the sausages after 1 day or mature them for up to 48 hours for a 'sour' taste.

4 The sausages can either be grilled (in the entire string or individually), skewered on brochettes or deep-fried. To test they are cooked, prick them with a fork and if no fat bubbles out when the fork is removed, they are cooked. If you are deep-frying, prick the skin in several places before plunging into hot oil. Serve with sprigs of fresh coriander, fine slivers of fresh ginger, ground roasted peanuts and finely chopped small fresh red or green chillies.

beef curry with bamboo shoots gaeng normai nua

This is another dish always made for temple festivals because it can be produced in quantity. It is offered to everyone: monks, the poor, any passers-by – even gawping tourists. Such acts are tamboon, which means they earn religious merit for those who do them. Appropriately, I last saw it being dished out at the Ban Ta Klang monk-making ceremony when the boys were being shaved and dressed prior to entering the monastery.

125ml (4fl oz) coconut cream
2 tablespoons vegetable oil
1 garlic clove, finely chopped
1 tablespoon red curry paste (see page 25)
2 tablespoons fish sauce
1 teaspoon granulated sugar
175g (6oz) tender beef steak, finely sliced
125ml (4fl oz) beef stock
2 kaffir lime leaves, roughly chopped
100g (4oz) bamboo shoots (see page 19), cut into slivers
20 fresh holy basil leaves

1 In a small pan, gently heat the coconut cream but do not let it boil. Remove from the heat, cover and set aside.

2 In a wok or frying pan, heat the oil and fry the garlic until golden brown. Add the curry paste and stir well. Pour in the warmed coconut cream and stir until it begins to reduce and thicken, then add the fish sauce and sugar.

3 Toss the beef into the pan and cook for 1 minute.

4 Pour in the stock and simmer for a further 2 minutes, or until the beef is just cooked through. In turn, stir in the lime leaves, bamboo shoots and basil leaves. Cook gently together for a final minute, then turn on to a serving dish.

grilled chicken with sweet chilli sauce gai yang

This used to be a uniquely north eastern speciality, but itinerant street sellers have spread it across the country. Still, as you drive across the invisible border into the province you know you're in Isan because you begin to see huge, brightly painted model chickens by the roadside, indicating the presence of a Gai Yang seller. If you stop, which you should, you'll probably find a clutch of lorry drivers perched on small stools around which live chickens forage for food, impervious to the diners salivating over chunks of golden chicken, grilled on slits of bamboo and served with hot and sweet sauce and a woven basket of sticky rice – delicious.

for the marinade

2 tablespoons sesame oil

2 garlic cloves, finely chopped

1 teaspoon finely chopped coriander root

2 small fresh red chillies, finely chopped

2 tablespoons fish sauce

1 teaspoon granulated sugar

400g (14oz) boneless chicken breasts, with skin, cut into chunks

for the hot and sweet sauce

6 tablespoons rice or white wine vinegar

4 tablespoons granulated sugar

1/2 teaspoon salt

2 garlic cloves, finely chopped

3 small fresh red chillies, finely chopped

1 In a large bowl, mix together all the ingredients for the marinade and leave to marinate for 30 minutes.

2 Meanwhile, make the hot and sweet sauce. In a small saucepan, heat the vinegar and sugar and stir until dissolved. Add the salt and simmer, stirring, until the liquid thickens. Remove from the heat, pour into a small bowl and leave to cool. When the sauce is cold, stir in the chopped garlic and chillies.

3 Preheat the grill to medium. Grill the marinated chicken for about 5 minutes on each side, or until cooked through.

4 Arrange the chicken on a platter and serve with the bowl of sauce.

papaya salad som tam

Now the most popular salad in Thailand – you see sellers squatting on the ground, pounding the ingredients everywhere, from garage forecourts to the entrances of grand hotels. There are countless versions and some highly specialised individual varieties. Even one of the present King's daughters, HRH Princess Mahachakri Sirindhorn, is known for her particular blend and she has written a popular song about it. I had a small part to play in popularising the dish when I started my first restaurant in London twenty years ago. Back then, it was commonly thought that *Som Tam* was too hot for foreigners, but I insisted on putting it on the menu and now its everywhere. If you order one from a street seller, nod or shake your head when the chillies start to go into the mortar, that way you won't end up with your head under a tap. This recipe contains a moderate number, so adjust up or down to taste.

2 garlic cloves, peeled

3–4 small fresh red or green chillies

2 long beans (see page 17), chopped into 5cm (2in) lengths

175g (6oz) fresh papaya, peeled, de-seeded and cut into fine slivers

1 tomato, cut into wedges

2 tablespoons fish sauce

1 tablespoon granulated sugar

2 tablespoons lime juice

to serve

a selection of fresh firm green vegetables in season – iceberg lettuce, cucumber, white cabbage, and so on

1 Pound the garlic in a large mortar, then add the chillies and pound again. Add the long beans, breaking them up slightly. Now take a spoon and stir in the papaya. Lightly pound together, then stir in the tomato and lightly pound again.

2 Add the fish sauce, sugar and lime juice, stirring well, then turn into a serving dish. Serve with fresh raw vegetables – any leaves, such as white cabbage, can be used as a scoop for the spicy mixture.

Young green papaya.

spicy chicken salad laab gai

This is basic peasant food in Isan as well as Laos, whose people are ethnically the same. *Laab* can be made from any sort of ground ingredients mixed with spices. In Laos the main flavouring is often fish pickle, to help 'down' the sticky rice. Both there and in Isan it is often served with raw plants, usually picked in the wild around the villages, and lightly cooked vegetables. You can make *Laab* with everything from beef and duck to fish and frog, so although I've played safe with chicken, do adapt as you wish.

for the chicken

175g (6oz) minced chicken

2 teaspoons finely chopped galangal (see page 17)

2 tablespoons fish sauce

2 tablespoons lime juice

1 teaspoon granulated sugar

1/2 teaspoon chilli powder

5 small shallots, thinly sliced

4 spring onions, finely chopped

2 teaspoons dry-fried rice (see page 29)

20 fresh mint leaves

to serve

a selection of raw crisp green vegetables, such as long beans, morning
   glory and white cabbage

1 Place the minced chicken in a heavy-based saucepan and heat while stirring in the galangal, fish sauce, lime juice, sugar and chilli powder. Continue to stir-fry until the meat is cooked through.

2 Remove the pan from the heat and stir in the shallots, spring onions, dry-fried rice and mint leaves.

3 Turn on to a serving dish and serve with a selection of raw crisp green vegetables.

fried marinated beef nua kem

(serves 4 – see page 14)

4 tablespoons fish sauce

2 teaspoons granulated sugar

1 tablespoon vegetable oil, plus 6 tablespoons for frying

450g (1lb) skirt or flank of beef, sliced diagonally across the grain into
   8–10 pieces

1 Combine the fish sauce, sugar and 1 tablespoon of oil in a bowl. Add the pieces of beef and turn them thoroughly in the mixture. Leave to marinate for at least 1 hour.

2 Remove the meat from the bowl and leave to drain overnight on a wire rack. Discard the marinade.

3 To cook the beef, heat 6 tablespoons oil in a frying pan until a very light haze appears. Add the beef and fry for about 5 minutes on each side, or until dark golden brown. Serve.

beef and vegetable noodles with black beans sen mee lahd nah

2 tablespoons vegetable oil

225g (8oz) soaked *sen mee* noodles (see page 24), drained and separated

1 tablespoon light soy sauce

1 garlic clove, finely chopped

100g (4oz) beef steak, finely sliced

1 tablespoon fish sauce

about 4 tablespoons beef stock, plus extra if necessary

1 teaspoon black bean sauce

1 teaspoon plain flour mixed with 4 tablespoons water to make a thin
   paste (this will give more than you need)

100g (4oz) mixed green vegetables (spring greens, mangetout, broccoli,
   for example)

¹/₂ teaspoon granulated sugar

¹/₄ teaspoon ground white pepper

1 In a wok or frying pan, heat 1 tablespoon oil. Add the noodles and stir-fry quickly to prevent them from sticking. Add the soy sauce and stir-fry for 30–60 seconds. Turn on to a serving dish, keep warm and set aside.

2 Add the remaining oil to the wok and fry the garlic until golden brown. Add the beef and stir-fry over a high heat until the meat loses its red colour. Stir in the fish sauce, a little stock and the black bean sauce. Thicken with a little of the flour and water mixture, stirring all the time to prevent lumps forming. Toss in the vegetables and sugar and stir-fry for a few seconds. Season with pepper, stir once, then pour over the noodles and serve.

skewered marinated pork moo ping

This makes about 8 skewers, so have 10 available. Try to find 15–20cm (6–8in) wooden skewers.

for the pork marinade

2 garlic cloves, finely chopped

6 coriander roots, finely chopped

4 tablespoons fish sauce

1 tablespoon light soy sauce

125ml (4fl oz) thick coconut cream

1 tablespoon vegetable oil

1 tablespoon granulated sugar

1/2 teaspoon ground white pepper

450g (1lb) lean pork, thinly sliced into 4 x 7.5cm (1 1/2 x 3in) pieces

for the chilli sauce

1 tablespoon fish sauce

2 tablespoons lemon juice

1 tablespoon light soy sauce

1 teaspoon chilli powder

1 tablespoon granulated sugar

1 tablespoon fresh coriander, coarsely chopped

1 Combine all the ingredients for the marinade in a bowl and mix together well together, making sure that each piece of meat is thoroughly coated. Leave to marinate for at least 30 minutes.

2 While the meat is marinating, place all the sauce ingredients in a small bowl and mix well. Taste and if the sauce is too hot, add more fish sauce, lemon juice and sugar. Set aside.

3 Preheat the grill to high. Thread 2 pieces of meat on to each skewer, making sure that as much of the meat as possible will be exposed to the grill.

4 Grill for 2–3 minutes on each side, or until the meat is thoroughly cooked through. Serve on a dish garnished with lettuce, parsley or coriander, with the sauce on the side.

pork toasts kanom bung na moo

Makes about 20 toasts

I last saw this in Surin market, made with long French baguettes, which probably means that the vendor was originally from Cambodia or Laos where they continue to make fresh French bread daily, as in the colonial era. It is best to use slightly stale bread, so it won't soak up too much oil when it's being deep-fried.

5 slices day-old bread

2 garlic cloves, finely chopped

3 coriander roots, chopped

100g (4oz) minced pork

2 eggs

2 tablespoons fish sauce

a pinch of ground white pepper

1 tablespoon milk or cold water

vegetable oil for deep-frying

to garnish

fresh coriander leaves, quartered cucumber, finely sliced rings of fresh red and green chilli

1 Preheat the oven to 120°C/250°F/gas mark ¹/₂. Trim the crusts off the bread and cut each slice into 4 quarters (or cut into decorative shapes using a pastry cutter). Lay the pieces on a baking sheet and bake in the oven for about 10 minutes, or until the bread starts to crisp. Remove from the oven.

2 Meanwhile, pound the garlic and coriander roots in a mortar. Transfer to a mixing bowl and combine with the minced pork, 1 egg, the fish sauce and the ground white pepper. Mix thoroughly. Place a scant teaspoon of the mixture on each piece of toast and spread it across the surface. Combine the remaining egg with the milk or water, and brush lightly over each pork toast.

3 Heat the oil in a deep-fryer to 200°C (400°F) and fry the toasts, a few at a time, for 2–3 minutes until golden brown. Drain on kitchen paper, then arrange on a large plate. Garnish with coriander leaves, cucumber or chilli, or a mixture of all three pierced with a toothpick. Serve with fresh cucumber pickle (*Adjahd*, see page 52).

jungle curry gaeng pah nua

The most obvious difference between this typical Isan curry and those from further south is that it doesn't use coconut milk or cream, the palm being a coastal plant. They also use particular vegetables, which in the original would probably have been growing wild. And lastly, there's the hot spiciness, which is meant to help 'down' large quantities of sticky rice.

2 tablespoons vegetable oil

1 garlic clove, finely chopped

1 tablespoon red curry paste (see page 25)

175g (6oz) lean beef steak, finely sliced

about 225ml (8fl oz) water

2 tablespoons fish sauce

^{1}/$_2$ teaspoon granulated sugar

10 slivers of krachai (see page 17), if using dried, soak in water for
   10–15 minutes to soften

100g (4oz) prepared vegetables (such as 6 thin green beans, trimmed
   and cut into 2.5cm (1in) pieces; 1 small carrot, slivered; 2 small green
   aubergines, quartered)

12–15 fresh holy basil leaves

2 whole fresh green peppercorns, or 15 dried black peppercorns

3 kaffir lime leaves, finely chopped

1 In a wok or frying pan, heat the oil and fry the garlic until golden brown. Add the curry paste and stir-fry together for 5–10 seconds. Add the slices of steak and stir-fry for a further 10 seconds. Stir in 2 tablespoons water, the fish sauce, sugar and krachai, cooking for a few seconds more.

2 Toss in the prepared vegetables with the remaining water, basil leaves, peppercorns and chopped lime leaves. Stir for a few seconds (just long enough to cook the vegetables, which should retain their crispness).

3 Turn into a bowl and serve.

The author with another greedy elephant.

duck with tamarind sauce ped makarm

for the marinade

1 garlic clove, finely chopped

1 teaspoon finely chopped coriander root

1 teaspoon coriander seeds

1 tablespoon fish sauce

1 teaspoon dark soy sauce

175g (6oz) duck breast

for the tamarind sauce

4 tablespoons water

150g (5oz) palm sugar (see page 20)

3 tablespoons fish sauce

2 tablespoons tamarind water (see page 21)

1/2 teaspoon chilli powder

to garnish

2 tablespoons vegetable oil

3 small shallots, finely sliced

1 Mix all the ingredients for the marinade together in a bowl, add the duck breast and coat well. Leave to marinate for 1 hour.

2 Make the tamarind sauce. In a small frying pan, heat together the water and palm sugar, stirring constantly. Add the fish sauce, tamarind water and chilli powder, stirring until the sauce thickens slightly. Leave to cool, then pour into a small bowl and set aside.

3 Make the garnish. In a small frying pan, heat the oil and fry the shallots until golden brown. Remove the shallots with a slotted spoon and set aside.

4 Place the marinated duck breast under a preheated hot grill and grill for 4–5 minutes on each side. Discard the marinade.

5 Cut the duck into thin slices and arrange on a serving dish. Pour the tamarind sauce over the duck and garnish with the crispy shallots.

sliced steak with hot and sour sauce nua yang

This is very easy to make. In Isan they would probably use water buffalo – and they'd use every morsel, from the intestines to the sexual organs – but here we're going for a simple beef steak.

175g (6oz) lean beef steak
1 tablespoon lemon juice
1 tablespoon fish sauce
1 teaspoon granulated sugar
1/2 teaspoon chilli powder
2 shallots, finely sliced
1 small spring onion, chopped

to serve
lettuce, finely sliced carrot and slices of English cucumber

to garnish
1 sprig of fresh coriander, coarsely chopped

1 Arrange the lettuce, carrot and cucumber on a serving plate and set aside.

2 Preheat the grill. When it is really hot, grill the steak so that the meat remains rare on the inside, turning once. Slice thinly and set aside.

3 In a bowl, mix together the lemon juice, fish sauce, sugar and chilli powder. Add the shallots, spring onion and slices of cooked beef. Stir quickly, then turn on to the serving dish and garnish with fresh coriander.

thai dim sum khanom jeeb

Makes 15

This is a Thai version of the classic Chinese *dim sum*, testimony to the connections between southern China, Laos and across the Mekong into Isan. The numbers of itinerant Chinese traders and transporters inevitably means enterprising street vendors will try to satisfy their needs by cooking Chinese food, even if the dishes get transformed into distinctly local specialities.

for the dim sum

225g (8oz) minced pork

60g (2oz) raw prawns, peeled, de-veined and finely chopped

30g (1oz) water chestnuts (see page 21), finely chopped

1 tablespoon fish sauce

1 tablespoon light soy sauce

1 tablespoon oyster sauce

¹/₂ teaspoon gound white pepper

1 teaspoon granulated sugar

15 sheets won ton pastry

for the garlic oil

2 tablespoons vegetable oil

2 large garlic cloves, finely chopped

for the chilli sauce

1 tablespoon dark soy sauce

2 tablespoons light soy sauce

2 tablespoons rice or white wine vinegar

2 teaspoons granulated sugar

2 small fresh red chillies, finely chopped

1 spring onion, finely chopped

1 Mix all the ingredients for the dim sum, except for the won ton pastry, together in a bowl and set aside.

2 Make the garlic oil. In a small frying pan, heat the oil and fry the garlic until golden brown. Set aside to infuse, reserving both the oil and the garlic.

3 Make a circle of the thumb and forefinger of 1 hand. Lay a won ton pastry sheet over the circle and press the middle to make a little 'sack'. Place about 1 tablespoon of the filling mixture inside the 'sack', then lightly squeeze the top edges of the pastry sheet together to contain the mixture, leaving the top open. Repeat to make 15 dim sum.

4 Place the prepared dim sum in a steamer and steam for 10 minutes.

5 Meanwhile, make the chilli sauce by combining all the ingredients in a small bowl. Pour the reserved garlic and oil into a separate bowl.

6 Transfer the cooked dim sum to a plate and serve with the chilli sauce and garlic oil.

fried catfish with krachai
pad pet pla duk

The Mekong, which forms the frontier between Laos and Isan, also provides plentiful supplies of catfish, which has a flavour quite different from more common sea fish. If you have a good fishmonger, you could experiment with whatever river fish is available or better still, go fishing yourself.

1 whole catfish, weighing about 275g (10oz) or the equivalent available freshwater fish such as trout

vegetable oil for deep-frying, plus 1 tablespoon extra for stir-frying

1 tablespoon red curry paste (see page 25)

4 tablespoons coconut cream

2 tablespoons (approx. 3 small rhizomes) krachai ('lesser' garlic – see page 20), slivered into fine matchsticks

2 tablespoons fish sauce

1 tablespoon granulated sugar

3 kaffir lime leaves, rolled into a cigarette shape and finely slivered across

2 large fresh red chillies, sliced into ovals

1   Clean the fish and pat dry, then cut across into 2.5cm (1in) slices.

2   Heat the oil in a deep-fryer to 200°C (400°F).

3   Deep-fry the fish slices until hard but not yet crispy. Drain on kitchen paper and set aside.

4   In a wok or frying pan, heat 1 tablespoon oil, add the red curry paste and stir well until it begins to blend with the oil – 2–3 seconds. Add half the coconut cream and stir well, then add the deep-fried fish and coat with the mixture. Stir in the remaining coconut cream, then add the krachai, fish sauce, sugar, lime leaves and chillies, stirring between each addition. Turn on to a dish and serve.

spicy pork noodles with basil leaf
gueyteow pad ki mow

1 tablespoon vegetable oil

1 garlic clove, finely chopped

1–2 small fresh red chillies, finely chopped

100g (4oz) lean pork, thinly sliced

2 tablespoons fish sauce

1/2 teaspoon granulated sugar

10 fresh basil leaves (kaffir lime leaves can also be used)

1 medium tomato, chopped

225g (8oz) (wet weight) soaked *sen yai* noodles (see page 24), rinsed
 and separated

to garnish
fresh coriander, coarsely chopped

1 In a wok or frying pan, heat the oil and fry the garlic until golden brown.
Add the chillies and stir for 2 seconds, then add the pork and stir-fry for a
couple more seconds to seal the juices.

2 Add the fish sauce, sugar and basil or lime leaves, stirring quickly after
each addition. Add the tomato, stir until cooked, then add the noodles.
Continue to stir-fry over a high heat until the pork is cooked through.

3 Turn on to a serving dish and garnish with fresh coriander. If using
lime leaves, you may wish to remove them before serving as they can be
quite tough.

fried egg noodles with beancurd
ba mee pad tao hou

2 tablespoons vegetable oil

1 garlic clove, finely chopped

1 egg

60g (2oz) ready-fried beancurd (see page 19), chopped into 2.5cm (1in)
 cubes

1 nest *ba mee* (egg) noodles, dipped in boiling water until just cooked,
 then drained (see page 24)

1 tablespoon preserved vegetable (*tang chi* , see page 21), finely chopped

1 tablespoon light soy sauce

1 teaspoon granulated sugar

60g (2oz) beansprouts

2 spring onions, cut into 2.5cm (1in) lengths

1 tablespoon crushed roasted peanuts

1/2 teaspoon chilli powder

1 tablespoon lemon juice

1 Heat the oil in a wok or frying pan, add the garlic and fry until
golden brown.

2 Break the egg into the pan, leave to set for a moment, then stir.

3 Add the beancurd with the cooked noodles and combine well.

4 Stir in the preserved turnip, soy sauce, sugar, beansprouts, spring
onions, crushed peanuts, chilli powder and lemon juice. Transfer to a
serving dish and serve.

Ba mee or egg noodles.

fried vermicelli with pork and spring onions pad wun sen

Because these noodles are long, they're always associated with long life. The dish is not chilli hot so it can be eaten by anyone, including little children, which is why you always see it being served up at village festivals like the monk-making celebrations at the elephant village of Ban Ta Klang – of course the wandering elephants are always trying to steal some.

60g (2oz) wun sen noodles (see page 24), soaked in cold water for
   15 minutes
2 tablespoons vegetable oil
1 garlic clove, finely chopped
100g (4oz) lean pork, finely sliced
1 tablespoon fish sauce
2 tablespoons light soy sauce
1 egg
2 tablespoons pork or chicken stock or water
1 small onion, slivered
6–8 dried mushrooms, soaked in cold water until soft (about 15 minutes),
   drained and cut in half if very large
2 spring onions, trimmed and cut into 4cm (1½in) lengths
½ teaspoon granulated sugar
ground white pepper, to season

1 Drain the noodles ready for cooking. Set aside.

2 In a wok or frying pan, heat the oil and fry the garlic until golden brown. Add the pork and stir-fry briefly until the meat is opaque. Add the fish sauce and 1 tablespoon soy sauce and stir. Break the egg into the pan and spread it around to cook it a little.

3 Add the drained noodles and mix thoroughly. Add the remaining soy sauce, the stock or water, onion and mushrooms and stir quickly to mix well. Toss in the spring onions, sugar and a sprinkling of white pepper, stir once more and turn on to a serving dish.

The author buying food from a *hahp* seller, watched
over by a cut-out portrait of the king.

spring rolls po pea tod

This 'Chinese' dish, or more precisely a Vietnamese/Chinese version of the classic Chinese dish, was probably brought to Thailand by refugees crossing into Isan during the communist era, many of whom opened restaurants. Actually, I think the Vietnamese food in Thailand is better than in Vietnam itself, since so many restaurateurs were among the small businessmen who were forced to flee. I also think the adaptations to Thai taste improved dishes such as this – but then I would, wouldn't I? However, accompanying any dish with so much fresh salad and vegetables is typically Vietnamese.

for the dipping sauces
4 tablespoons granulated sugar

6 tablespoons rice or white wine vinegar

1/2 teaspoon salt

1 small fresh red chilli, finely chopped

1 small fresh green chilli, finely chopped

for the spring rolls
2 tablespoons plain flour

4 tablespoons water

6 spring roll sheets (see page 21), 25cm (10in) square

100g (4oz) *wun sen* noodles (see page 24), soaked

8 pieces dried black fungus mushroom (see page 17), soaked in cold
  water to soften, drained and chopped very finely

100g (4oz) minced pork

2 garlic cloves, finely chopped

2 tablespoons fish sauce

2 tablespoons light soy sauce

1/2 teaspoon granulated sugar

1/2 teaspoon ground white pepper

vegetable oil for deep-frying

1 First make the dipping sauces. Place the sugar and vinegar in a small pan and heat gently, stirring, until the sugar has dissolved. Add the salt, bring to the boil and boil rapidly until the sauce thickens. Divide between 2 bowls and stir the chopped chillies into one of them. Set aside.

2 Make the spring rolls. Combine the flour and water in a small saucepan and heat gently, stirring all the time until thick and clear. Pour into a saucer and set aside.

3 Cut each spring roll sheet into 4 quarters and set aside.

4 Drain the noodles and, using scissors, chop them up into very small pieces. Place in a mixing bowl with the finely chopped mushroom, minced pork, garlic, fish sauce, soy sauce, sugar and a shaking of white pepper. Combine well.

5 Place the quarters of spring roll pastry on a work surface and place a heaped teaspoon of the filling on each. Fold in 3 corners to make an envelope shape and wrap tightly, rolling towards the open corner. Brush a little of the flour and water paste on the open corner and fold it over to seal. At this point, the rolls can be chilled or frozen for future use.

6 To cook, heat the oil in a deep-fryer to 200°C (400°F) or in a deep sauce pan until a light haze appears. Deep-fry the rolls until golden brown, drain on kitchen paper and serve on a plate with the 2 dipping sauces.

index